'I am happy to give this book a stupendous five-star endorsement – it is the book we all need to change our inner and outer life when we feel stuck in this world of crisis. It is clear, inspiring, and full of actionable wisdom. Ed's voice of kindness, as well as his kick-up-the-ass attitude that we all need, runs so clearly through it.'

Julia Samuel MBE, best-selling author of *Grief Works*

'Ed is a brilliant coach. He walked by my side when my company took off, enabling me to live my own version of a successful life instead of the one that the world had outlined for me.'

Frederic Kerrest, Co-Founder and COO of Nasdaq-listed Okta

'This book commands your attention, and appeals to anyone who wants to move their life forward and follow their dreams. Ed's conviction and positive energy shines through, spurring you on and willing you to give it everything you've got.'

Thomasina Miers OBE, cook, author and Co-Founder of Wahaca

'Modern life isn't easy to navigate. Even harder is navigating it in a way that feels meaningful, balanced and joyful. *The Modern Maverick* provides a clear and helpful approach. It asks you to be honest with yourself about what matters and how you are doing, and it helps you let go of distracting expectations so you can begin to figure out your own idea of success. It offers deep guidance on focusing your time and creating the right habits, and contains quiet and much-needed wisdom for our noisy times.'

Shamil Thakrar, Co-Founder and CEO, Dishoom

'Invest in this book to invest in yourself. It will be worth it. Well-written, clear, deep and pragmatic. The combination of personal stories, excellent ideas and exercises is just right. Take this challenge on and your life will be the better for it.'

Dr Carol Kauffman, Assistant Professor at Harvard,
Founder Institute of Coaching, Thinkers 50 top 8 coaches
and ranked #1 Leadership Coach by Marshall Goldsmith MG100

'If I can claim the title "Modern Maverick", then it is thanks to Ed's coaching. This book brilliantly lays out the Maverick Way that Ed has developed and applied so effectively to me, as well as many other entrepreneurs. It gives us the tools to live our best lives, true to ourselves, and guides us to find our own version of success. *The Modern Maverick* is as important to the 2020s as The Age of Unreason was in the 1990s. Both Ed Haddon and Charles Handy, respectively, have seen into the future and given us a playbook of how to live our best lives in the coming decades.'

Simon Hill-Norton, Co-Founder of Sweaty Betty

'Ed and his team have been an important part of the success of Hawksmoor. Talent and hard work will get you so far, but, as in sports, top quality coaching makes a huge difference. *The Modern Maverick* is a great resource for replicating that coaching in your own career or business.'

Will Beckett, Co-Founder and CEO of Hawksmoor

'With toes over the edge of a life-changing career change, I turned to Ed for the wise counsel of a trusted friend. It was a timely intervention. No one is watching your movie. Once you release yourself from the expectations you think others have of you and decide on what brings you joy, you tap into what makes you magic. You do you. Thank you Ed for the nudge of a lifetime. I could have done with this book sooner!'

Demetra Pinsent, CEO of Charlotte Tilbury

'This book will help unlock any limiting beliefs you may have around success and what is possible, allowing you to live a freer, happier and more fulfilled life. It is a call to action and a really practical framework to effect the change you seek.'

ounder of Finisterre

'As an honorary Maverick, I would highly recommend having a read of this wonderful collection of insights into why we might be finding life a bit of a slog, and what we can do about it. Ed has put together the tools for you to create your own map and define your own success. A necessary book in this time of uncertainty.'

Pippa Evans, Co-Founder of The Sunday Assembly and author of *Improv your Life*

'Ed's coaching has inspired so many people. This is an important book. It has so much wisdom in it, whether you are searching for meaning, growing a company, or seeking to contribute to a community.'

Henry Dimbleby MBE, Co-Founder of Leon and author of the National Food Strategy

'If you feel it's impossible to make your own choices in your work, in your life and in our world, read *The Modern Maverick*. Happily, you can make your own choices. This book – inspiringly and practically – shows you how.'

James Harding, Founder and editor of Tortoise Media and former editor of *The Times*

'No surprise that Ed has written a book about the maverick plan – I've never known anyone as content with the new path onto which he has steered. Calm, unflustered and confident in his professional choices and reaping the internal rewards from it.'

Sir Matthew Pinsent, four-time Olympic Gold Medallist

'It's a dream for many people to combine their work with their personal passion. Finding work that doesn't feel like work and using your unique talents to pursue an inspiring and authentic vision is deeply fulfilling. But how do you know where to start on that journey? Ed's book gives you the tools and confidence to take the first step towards a better, more fulfilling life. It's the ideal companion for anyone looking to start their own journey.'

Simon Mottram, Founder of Rapha

'Ed Haddon develops an ancient realisation; that we humans have an inner voice which can be an invaluable guide, and shows us how we can detect, follow and work with it. He knows that we need assistance because the path that unfolds can be tricky, mostly because it is not borrowed or imitated, but unique. Socrates had his daemon. Shakespeare spoke of conscience as the god within the breast. Ed shows us practical ways to converse with your inner maverick.'

Dr Mark Vernon, author and psychotherapist

'Working with Ed Haddon has been transformational. He has super-charged my growth, and helped keep me sane through some of the most challenging moments of my career – something I'll always be grateful for. This book opens up Ed's extraordinary toolkit, built upon many decades of learning and experience.'

Paul Croft, Co-Founder of Mediatonic (now part of Epic Games)

'I've been working with Ed for four years, through some incredibly tough times and what most people would call, a fantastic exit. This has not been easy, but with his Maverick coaching, we got there. You can do it too. *The Modern Maverick* is a blueprint for a better life, and a stronger, more fulfilled self, who can go on and achieve what is really important to you, and to the world.'

Phil Chambers, Co-Founder of Peakon (now part of Workday)

THE MODERN MAVERICK

Why writing your own rules is better for you, your work and the world

ED HADDON

BLOOMSBURY BUSINESS
LONDON • OXFORD • NEW YORK • NEW DELHI • SYDNEY

BLOOMSBURY BUSINESS
Bloomsbury Publishing Plc
50 Bedford Square, London, WC1B 3DP, UK
29 Earlsfort Terrace, Dublin 2, Ireland

BLOOMSBURY, BLOOMSBURY BUSINESS and the Diana logo are trademarks of Bloomsbury Publishing Plc

First published in Great Britain 2023

A catalogue record for this book is available from the British Library

Library of Congress Cataloguing-in-Publication data has been applied for

ISBN: 978-1-3994-0709-0; eBook: 978-1-3994-0705-2

2 4 6 8 10 9 7 5 3 s1

Typeset by Deanta Global Publishing Services, Chennai, India
Printed and bound in Great Britain by CPI Group (UK) Ltd, Croydon CR0 4YY

FSC www.fsc.org MIX Paper | Supporting responsible forestry FSC® C171272

To find out more about our authors and books visit www.bloomsbury.com and sign up for our newsletters

For Jo, Tessa, Alice, Joe, and all you other Mavericks

Contents

Acknowledgements

This book originated in early conversations over two decades ago, with long-suffering friends talking about happy gardeners and the four table legs of happiness. Thank you to all of you who endured my ramblings.

Sacha Bonsor battled through a very early draft and has been invaluable as the book has taken shape and developed. James Harding was an early reader of the proposal and focused me in on the 'define your own success' theme. Julia Samuel provided counsel and wisdom in innumerate areas. Jeremy Houghton is a long-term enthusiast. The Neverns provided a unique and mainly unhelpful type of input.

Fiona Parashar is a brilliant coach and mentor. Her constant companionship and encouragement has made this journey possible. She also introduced me to the genius book coach Alison Jones. Without her boot camps and ongoing help you would not be reading this.

To my readers, your feedback was so invaluable and your time so appreciated; George Head, Camilla Campbell and Simon Hill-Norton. Kate Weinberg was insightful and warm at key moments.

To the team at Haddon Coaching. Nancy Wilde, Nick Thistleton, Clare Downes and Julian Mack who all helped shape and refine the content. Brilliant coaches and brilliant colleagues. I am so happy to be alongside you all and to take the Modern Maverick into the world with you. To Vanessa Locke for keeping us all on track.

To the incredible team at Bloomsbury. Ian Hallsworth to whom I will always be indebted for taking this project on and seeing the potential. Allie Collins for making it all happen. Jane Donovan for a brilliant copy edit. Aimee Knight and Rachel Nicholson have all played invaluable roles as the book has become a reality. Erin Brown and Mila Melia-Kapoor have done a great job of helping you find this book. And finally to Sutchinda Thompson for a wonderful cover design.

To my agent Jane Graham Maw for taking me on after a short phone call. I look forward to our conversations over the years to come. Toby Ingram provided the right words at the right time – his superpower. Andrew Franklin raised the bar, I look forward to jumping over it.

To Kathleen and her team at the best bookshop in the world (Toppings in Bath). Your enthusiasm for all books, and the thought of this one sitting on your hallowed shelves, has sustained me through some long shifts at the keyboard.

A big thank you to Cat Manson and Ailana Kamelmacher, both great storytellers, who helped think about the key messages in the book. Also to Natasha Fairweather who provided early motivation and clarity of purpose that kept me focused on why I was writing.

None of this is possible without a brilliant group of clients. It is a privilege to walk alongside you. You have taught me so much, and your contributions to this book are everywhere. To those that have provided case studies and more, you know who you are, thank you.

Finally to my family. The most important of all. My much missed Mum who started this and sowed the seeds of thinking about others. My sister Alice, who has always kept me honest. Our children May and Billy have enjoyed endless supplies of scrap paper thanks to the early drafts, and have been curious, interested and good levellers. My darling wife Jo, the expert author, thank you for your belief, encouragement and unwavering support. We are a great team.

To all the Mavericks listed above, and you the future Mavericks reading this, thank you for making me believe that this is worth fighting for.

Introduction

Is there a voice inside you that evokes a different life from the one you are living? Have you ever really stopped and listened to that voice? That voice is your Inner Maverick. If you have picked this book up, the chances are that voice is becoming louder and you are ready to listen. Your Inner Maverick speaks to a more independent life, a life of increased freedom and autonomy and uniqueness; stepping out of a box and standing apart from the crowd. A life of meaning that engages your unique talents in a way that helps rather than hinders, builds rather than consumes. A way of unlocking your life where you are more alive, happier, more fulfilled and those around you benefit exponentially.

This is hard to do in a society where we are pushed and pulled to conform. The modern triumvirate of education, advertising and capitalism combine to convince us that success is making money to live a life of material consumerism. Social media has poured petrol on this; the ability to compare ourselves to an infinitely curated universe creates a new level of need and envy. We neglect the all-important relationships in the real world, instead seeking 'likes' from people we will never or rarely meet in person. Work has come to dominate our waking hours and more and more people are struggling to find meaning there. However, we may be aware of a frontier on the edge of our thinking where we operate in a different way. But realizing this may be too complicated – we are too tired, it is too much like hard work, it is not clear and perhaps what we have now is not so bad after all. Making changes can be incredibly hard work, particularly when we are trying to do it on our own.

The Modern Maverick is about activating those instincts and listening to that inner voice, giving you the skills and ideas to create time to think clearly, to figure out the changes that need to be made and presenting you with the tools to make them happen. This book provides a framework that enables you to gain clarity, to find insights and to take action.

The longer we ignore the voice, the more deflated and defeated we can become. Our independent streak wears away and instead we find ourselves in a version of *The Truman Show*. In the film, Truman Burbank, played by Jim Carrey, begins to realize that he is a puppet being controlled by Christof, the director of the television show, and the hundreds of extras. His Inner Maverick begins to assert itself and in a poignant final scene, Truman chooses to leave the 'set' behind, walking through a door to a life unknown. The film's success resulted from a psychological connection with the longing for independence and autonomy of the audience.

The original mavericks were unbranded cattle that wandered off to join other herds and were seen as independent. These days the term is taken to mean someone who exhibits great independence in thought and action, or someone who holds unorthodox views. There is, however, something of a negative connotation of someone who acts wildly in a self-serving way. *The Modern Maverick* moves this on by recognizing the power of living in an autonomous way, living the life you love and believe, while at the same time contributing positively to those around you.

For Mavericks-in-waiting who want to listen to that voice and finally act, this book is for you. You are ready to explore and live by your own definition of success, not one borrowed from or implanted by society. And for those of you already on your Maverick Path who need a boost, and who are ready for the next level Maverick, then this book will help you achieve just that.

Your Legacy

This book is deeply practical. The aim is to help you coach yourself to a Maverick Life. Exercises are a key part of this, so let's start right now with one. Without thinking too much about it, write down the three-sentence eulogy that would be written about you today. Be honest.

....

....

Now, write down the three sentences you would *like* to be written about you when you do die.

....

....

What did you notice? Was there a big difference between the two? This book is about empowering you to close the gap between where you are now and where you want to be. It won't be easy; sometimes we start on the right path but stumble and at other times the path is not completely clear. This book will help, both in discovering your path and then staying on it.

You are likely to be functioning pretty well on a day-to-day level. You have adapted to find a place where you can make ends meet and get through your days and weeks. You may even experience fleeting moments of joy, but just not enough of them. Sometimes you feel trapped, living a life that others expected of you, but not the one you perhaps dreamt of for yourself. That annoying, soul-eroding itch will not go away, that feeling that you are capable of more than this, that you are able to do more for yourself, others and the world at large.

Along the Maverick Path is the magic of really taking time to understand and explore your superpower. It unlocks life, like new levels on a computer game. You benefit by finding your sweet spot, and crucially those around you gain from being around a happier, energetic and more giving version of you.

The Modern Maverick sets out to answer three questions:

1) What does it mean to be a Maverick today?
2) Why does it matter?
3) How can you live a Maverick Life?

Let's start by looking at the set of ideas that define a Modern Maverick:

- We overcome the fear and challenge of change through gradual transition, experiments and side hustle, building experience and confidence as we walk our Maverick Path.
- We know that our own happiness and fulfilment relies on positive relationships with our clan, our community and our world.
- We remember that the gravitational pull of society towards materialism and individualism is strong. Without ongoing thought and attention, we default to unhealthy thinking and action.
- Our ability to think clearly, to create our Maverick Path and then make it happen, relies on us looking after ourselves, on being Life Fit. We need full batteries.
- We all have a calling and a voice, but they are sometimes hard to find and even harder to dedicate ourselves to. If we keep ignoring them, we pass a point of no return where our energy is spent and we live out a life of frustration and futility, an insult to our Inner Maverick.
- Deep honesty and vulnerability with ourselves and others are the rocky steep road to finding our Maverick Path.

- When thinking about giving our energy and spirit, we start with those who are closest and most vulnerable: children if we have them, elderly relatives, our friends, our community. Only then do we think about our other work, our 'job'. This is the inverse of our default mode that has been shaped by our education and the media.
- When we pursue money, power and medals, we should be asking ourselves, who are we doing this for? Is this the best use of our precious time and energy?
- We make our decisions based on what we know in our hearts is who we are, not on what we feel we should be, ought to do or do without thinking.
- We build and live our own definition of success, focusing on what matters to us, what makes us grow and sing.
- By using 'could' rather than 'should', we create lives that are better for ourselves, others and the world.
- We work hard on our habits and skills to enable us to live in the sweet spot between idleness and burnout with high energy levels.
- We seek autonomy so that we can pursue our Maverick Path. Change, progress and fulfilment are intentional.
- We cannot do this alone; we need others to help us on our Maverick Path and we assemble this team.
- We recognize that we are all being called – we need to make changes to ensure the next generations survive.

Some of these points may resonate, some you may agree with, while others might seem alien or out of reach. This book explores these principles in more detail and sets out arguments and ideas to help you on your way. The *idea* of the life you love is important, but making it happen is the really hard part.

The Gross Domestic Product experiment of the last 40 years has had too few winners and left the rest of us wondering if we have been chasing the wrong definition of success. On top of that, the world urgently needs us at our best, doing meaningful work that is in some way contributing to the survival and flourishing of mankind. That means we need to be more entrepreneurial in our approach to life, creating the autonomy to allocate the scarce resource of our time and energy into a high-impact life that not only benefits ourselves, but more crucially those around us and the world at large.

If we continue sleepwalking through excess consumption, mundane jobs and hyper individualization, the path is pretty clear. Our democracies will fail, our planet will stop supporting us and we will have squandered our talents and resources. Our Inner Maverick is telling us that we are not on the right track, at an individual and societal level. For some it will be a small evolution, for others a major revolution. What matters is that we act now.

What's in This Book?

The following chapters will take you through a four-step process to living your Maverick Life. There is a mix of searching questions, case studies, accessible psychology, Olympic principles, exercises and ideas from other Mavericks. *The Modern Maverick* is your coach and the exercises are there to hold you to account, to help you develop your own ideas and actions. This book aims to be different, not just picking up ideas and thinking but taking those ideas into the world, testing and refining.

Part I: Discover **– Defining your version of success.** What does success look like for you? Unless you have ownership of what success means to you, it is impossible to live a conscious Maverick Life. This involves turning your mind from what others might think, from an externally generated idea of success and towards your inner voice. What really matters to you? What has shaped you? What role does your ego play? Take an honest look at your life now. How would you like to live and to die? This part ends with the Life Quotient (LQ) tool that helps you take stock of your life, the balance you currently have and looks at the idea of being Life Fit.

Part II: Dream – **How will you use your time?** What will you do with your time and energy? What are you uniquely put on this planet for? What are your superpowers and how do you use them? Who will benefit? For many, this is known simply as 'purpose'. This may include paid work, although not necessarily. Caring for others is an extremely high purpose but not always financially rewarding. This is about how you spend your days and who you spend them with. What do you do with the time when you are not working?

Part III: Do – **Performing at your best and becoming Life Fit.** How do you recharge your batteries and make sure you are ready for the drive? How do you keep them charged and what can you do when they are running low? Doing any of this is hard; doing this when you are long-term tired, depressed or unhealthy is virtually impossible. Operating with depleted resources is very challenging and is one of the key impediments to change.

Part IV: Deepen – **Your Maverick Plan.** Putting together a plan, running experiments, measuring what happens and then refining the plan can be challenging. There is, after all, a reason why you are reading this book. The book is here to help, where previously you may have turned away or ignored the voice. There are aspects of your character that will get in the way. Limiting beliefs that mean even if you have a plan, you do not start on it, or you grind to a halt at the first speed bump. The plan will not proceed to plan. Some things will work and can be doubled down on, others will fail and can be analysed with curiosity rather than judgement. The book does not leave you with a vague notion of success or higher purpose but a clear plan and an approach that harnesses your own capabilities so that you can make that plan work.

How to Use This Book

Some people will want to read the book straight through, from beginning to end – and that can often be a great way to approach things. For others, the different sections can be dipped in and out of – if there's a particular part that calls to you, feel free to start there. Doing the LQ exercise at the end of Part I (see page 35) and using it to guide you through Part III (pages 91–189) will offer some quick wins on key subjects that are helpful, even if you do not wish to undertake the whole Maverick journey.

I have not included footnotes as I feel these might disrupt your reading flow. Instead, there is a full set of references, as well as some suggested reading at the end of the book. Names have been changed in case studies to protect identities, except where full names are used as clients have expressed a wish to be identified.

As for the interactive parts, I know it can be tempting not to do the exercises; I personally grimace when I come across them in books. If this is you, then I understand. But without the exercises, the book becomes an interesting yet inconsequential read. Change will not happen and you will remain where you are. However, the exercises will help to unlock your life and assist you in developing your Maverick Life. They enable you to build a life you love and believe in, and to bring about change in the world around you. They are worth the effort.

You can jot down some ideas in the spaces provided, although I would recommend buying a wonderful notebook, a special pen or having your keyboard to hand if you are a digital thinker. There is a Modern Maverick website which you can access (www.themodernmaverick.com) and you'll be able to complete some of the exercises there, allowing you to store and update answers over time.

If I was working with you one-to-one as your coach, I would hold you accountable and follow up with you on each session to help you reflect on your progress and really take an active part in shaping your life. This book is your coach and you will discover how to engage the help of others – you really do not have to do this alone. The research from the American Society of Training and Development is unequivocal on this: if you find yourself an accountability partner, then your chances of making your goals happen shoot up to 95 per cent. So start thinking now about who this might be. Could you both read the book and hold each other accountable?

Another way to turn this from a passive reading experience into an active, life-building experience is to use the reflection/summary space at the end of each chapter for you to summarize what you take from that piece of the process. If you have read this type of book before, then you will know how easy it is to finish the last page and then do nothing. Filling in the exercises and summaries as you go ensures this will not happen.

There are some sections that I believe are more key than others and you will see those in bold in the table of contents at the beginning. If you want to dip in, rather than reading top to bottom, start with these as a guide. At times I will put forward some ideas and thoughts with conviction. I apologize in advance if in any way this makes you feel judged. It is hard to present definitive ideas without people feeling somehow criticized. Please take that feeling as an opportunity to ask yourself good questions and of course reject the ideas if they really do not resonate with you. The power of coaching is that the answers lie within you, the questions and exercises in this book are there to help you uncover those answers. I believe in you; this book is here to challenge and support, not judge.

My Story

You will see as you read through the book that I weave my own Maverick story into the text. I know from my coaching work that people can find carefully shared experience helpful. In sharing some of my life, I am hoping that you will find some resonance, company and ideas. I still feel the gravitational pull of societal expectations very heavily and often wonder if I am on the right path – there's no one who is convinced at all times that they have everything all worked out – but in clearer and more settled moments, I know that my Maverick Path is the right one.

My interest in people and what makes them tick started as a teenager, leading to an undergraduate degree in Psychology at Oxford University. I spent four years rowing competitively, including representing Great Britain at the Junior World Championships and the World Student Games. This experience taught me about the highs and lows of winning and failing. A short stint in the mainstream workforce, battling 50-hour weeks and zero autonomy, followed by an MBA from Harvard Business School, convinced me that I wanted to be my own boss in work and life, and that many people were sleepwalking into lives of corporate misery.

Twelve years as a struggling entrepreneur and early-stage investor showed me the dos and don'ts of having your own business, from both sides of the table. I still did not feel I was living my Maverick Life and I knew I hadn't figured out my superpower. But I battled on, stubbornly believing that I could make it work. In retrospect, life should never feel that hard for that long. I was doing the wrong work and it was at risk of damaging everything that was important to me – my reason for being, my health and my relationships. I was on the right pitch but playing in the wrong position.

In April 2006, I was fired from the company that I had spent the previous six years growing and struggling with. It really was rock bottom for me – my entrepreneurial dreams shattered, my plans of proposing to my then girlfriend wavering, no job to go to, no money and no clue how to move forward. I remember at the time someone said to me, 'This is the best thing that will ever happen to you.' I honestly felt like punching them! However, I know now how right they were: life was showing me that I was on the wrong path.

The penny finally dropped for me in 2008, when a coach helped me realize that my life's work was in enabling people to find the right work for them and their lives. It turned out my superpower was asking great questions and really being interested in the answers. It wasn't the daily operational work of building a company and leading a team which I had been fired from. Since then, I have trained and worked as a life coach, specializing in helping people find their Maverick within.

A Note About Privilege and Equality

It's worth noting at this point that I am a white middle-aged man of privilege. For ages, it seemed to me that I had only two choices: either I pull up the drawbridge and retire to the patriarchy, or I fall to the floor and endlessly apologize. However, I now hope and believe that there is a third choice, where I lower the drawbridge and walk out with a sense of curiosity, a knowledge that a fixed mindset is not going to help and a desire to listen and discuss. This book comes out of those ongoing discussions. If I misstep, as I am sure I do, then I apologize.

My language may seem clumsy at times, but I hope you will see that the Maverick Life is one of challenging the status quo, where we do not have to accept the way things are or have always been. This can only be a good thing for dismantling unequal power dynamics. Equal access to the things that matter is what is most important. The same false definition of success that lures us towards medals and money is also the one that defines and enables inequality, so let's get the success measures right and then make sure we democratize those measures. I know we can start a more transparent and fair access and allocation of all types of resource.

Now that we are ready to dive into the first steps on the Maverick Path, let me ask you to give three ratings on a scale of 1–10 for the questions below, 1 being low and 10 being high:

1. How ready are you to embark on this process?

....

2. How important is it to you to make these changes?

....

3. How confident are you that you can make these changes?

....

In Summary

You can now complete the summary box below. Over the page, you will be able to see my summary of the key points in this chapter, as well as some thoughts on the questions above.

My summary of this chapter...

1. ....

2. ....

3. ....

Key Points

1. The Modern Maverick looks for a more autonomous way of living, creating the life they love and believe in.

2. In doing so they benefit not just themselves but those around them and society at large; they change the world around them.

3. The exercises are a key part of the Maverick Path, find a way to do as many of them as you can.

If you scored yourself less than 7 on any of the rating questions above, it may be worth taking a pause, and reflecting on what might need to change before you go ahead. A low score would suggest that you are perhaps not ready to commit to the process just yet. I will ask you the same set of questions at the end of Chapter 14 – it will be interesting to compare the scores

PART I

Discover

CHAPTER ONE

Being Honest with Yourself

The first step to living a Maverick Life is making an honest assessment of who we are so that we can start to evolve and make changes. We all have stories and beliefs about ourselves. Some originate from when we were very young: 'I am the clumsy one', 'I am the loud one', 'I am the good one'. Some we build and groove as we grow older. We fight to hold onto our stories and in some extreme cases, we will die rather than dismantle the precarious scaffold for our identity that these stories represent. Stories can be helpful and empowering, or they can be debilitating, constantly holding us back; what is important for this chapter is that these stories can be examined and challenged, even modified or left behind completely. Positive stories can be amplified, turned into a touchstone for when times are challenging.

This is the point to stop reading if you are not interested in looking at your life closely.

Socrates is reported to have said: 'The unexamined life is not worth living.'

We will look through a kind lens – this is not about self-flagellation, after all – but nevertheless you will be making an honest assessment of where you are and what has helped and hindered you to date. One of the premises of the Maverick Path is that progress is impossible without first mapping the territory, so here is where we begin to open up to the idea and take some first steps.

So, now that we are ready to begin, how might you go about uncovering and annotating these stories? One way to start might be to take some time to write down what people would say about you or think about you. And you don't have to guess, asking those people is a good thing to do. In workplaces, 360-degree reviews are increasingly common. Asking for honest, sometimes anonymous, feedback on key behaviours or skills from colleagues who are above you, below you and alongside you works well when it comes to getting a clear picture of how you are seen. I have always wondered why this did not happen at home. Often I will ask clients to solicit honest feedback or opinions from those around them, based on how they are seen and how their actions are experienced.

Siblings and parents can be especially helpful here. After all, they have known you all your life and were often around and part of the formation of early stories. This is also a good pretext to have some honest conversations with your family.

Another interesting way of piecing stories together could be going back through old journals; sometimes your stories are hidden in plain sight. Here's an example: my wife loves to have people over to dinner, but she likes to be the one to do the cooking. This means that she can be on the edge of the conversation, listening rather than necessarily leading. She is an introvert and cooking in the background was her way of seeing friends and family without overloading her emotional state. After a bit of thinking she realized that one true story about her is this: 'I love gathering people, but do not like to be the centre of attention.' Fortunately, I am the opposite way round – so we work well together on this front.

My Stories

What are the three strongest stories that you tell about yourself, or that you hear others tell about you?

1. ....

2. ....

3. ....

What can you learn from these stories, how do they help you understand some of your behaviours?

An early client had been stuck since injuring his leg in a life-changing accident a few years previously. The story he told himself was that his leg prevented him from getting a job, or from moving on. When we really looked at this together, he began to see that his leg had become an excuse, a way of not confronting the future and the difficult choices that he faced. Awareness and questioning around this narrative freed him and he was able to start taking action and moving forward.

A practice of curious reflection and observation is to be one of the key recurring themes as we work through this book. Note that I have said curious, rather than judgemental. It's important that you resist making value judgements about yourself here; when we judge ourselves, we can reinforce the old stories and close ourselves down to change, growth or even compassion. If we can be *curious* about losing our temper, rather than labelling it a failure, we are likely to lose our temper less frequently. When working with clients, I am often pattern spotting, looking for what stands out. Almost always these patterns of behaviour or values seem totally normal to them. It is not until we put them in the spotlight that their unhelpfulness or value becomes clear.

These practices will take time to get to grips with and a lifetime to master so do not put too much pressure on yourself. Even the smallest increase in self-awareness can create a large shift in your state of mind and behaviour.

Take another look at the stories you have written down. Have you made any internal value judgements? If you have, try and rephrase the stories in a light of curiosity rather than judgement.

Although reflection starts with us holding a mirror up to ourselves, it does not have to be a solitary exercise. Maybe you have a coach or are thinking about finding one; it's not a necessity, but I certainly do encourage the idea. Alongside a formal coaching relationship, asking friends or family open questions can yield powerful answers. There are very few moments in life when we really glimpse what others truly think of us – perhaps an overheard conversation, a misaddressed email or a comment made in jest or anger. Those moments can be invaluable and need to be gently sought out and encouraged, rather than rejected.

Easily said, of course, and much less easily done. I know that I personally have an aversion to feedback. Even when it's not critical, it's not uncommon to find feedback in any form wildly uncomfortable. However, I recognize that, much like meditation or exercise, soliciting and integrating feedback is an essential life skill for the Maverick. In opening ourselves up to feedback, we become vulnerable and understandably this can lead to feeling defensive. Without it, though, we cannot grow and we do not work on our craft.

To make feedback easier to give or receive, you might consider using a principle often attributed to the thirteenth-century poet Rumi, who apparently offered three gates to pass though before telling someone a 'truth':

- Is it honest? (Most of us think this is enough)
- Is it necessary? (What is the intention of this, who is to benefit?)
- Is it kind? (Cruelty will ensure that the truth does not help.)

Asking others also helps protect us from wilful blindness. This is where our limiting beliefs prevent us from seeing or hearing the real facts. Limiting beliefs, often part of the stories we tell ourselves, are states of mind or beliefs about yourself that restrict you in some way. Some common limiting beliefs are:

- 'I'm not good enough'
- 'I don't have enough experience'
- 'I'm not smart enough'

Thinking this way keeps us stuck in a rut, unable to understand why we are closed to a way forward. We may start to blame others for our inertia and our falling behind. We may adopt a victim mentality, when in fact it is ourselves who are not confronting painful truths. Sometimes we imagine or misunderstand our position in the world. I often see this with clients who are talking about their own imposter syndrome. This is a massively common experience; a belief that we should not be where we are, or doing what we are doing, and that we will somehow be caught out.

When someone is experiencing this, I ask them to imagine being in a court of law in front of a judge. I ask them to act as the prosecutor in the case that they believe (e.g., I am not good enough). They present the facts of this case to the imaginary 'judge' and 'jury'. I take the opposite side and present evidence and facts that support the alternative narrative (e.g., you are good enough). I then ask them to assume the position of the judge and 'rule' on the case presented by the prosecutor. The client almost always throws the case out of court.

Here's an example: Megan claimed that people do not like her and that she has few real friends. I asked her to 'prosecute' this case in an imaginary court, so she presented the evidence that when she threw a party, several people did not come. She also added that she does not get invited to many dinners. In turn, I 'defended' the case, using as my evidence the point of view that over 50 people *did* attend her party. I also suggested that perhaps people were not having as many dinners as she imagined.

This is a simple but powerful exercise to help push through imposter syndrome, or an episode of wilful blindness – it's a way of shifting perspective. There is something comforting about sitting with our long-standing narratives and interpretations of events. Our Inner Maverick knows better, so let that person sit in the judge's seat and help break through some of the brick walls we put in place to keep us where we are.

Let's put this into practice…

Court of Law

Take one of your three stories above (see page 5) and use the Court of Law exercise. What would the prosecution say and what would the defence say? How would the judge rule?

Once you've tried it by yourself, think about trying it again with a friend or a loved one: do they rule differently to you?

What narrative has shifted for you after this exercise?

………………………………………………………………………………

………………………………………………………………………………

I use this exercise with clients extensively. We all construct false narratives, versions of events, that when examined under daylight fall apart. I encourage you to come back to your own court of law throughout the book. This is one of the key tools on the Maverick Path. We all fall into lazy thinking. Looking at the facts rather than the spin we put on them liberates us and frees up a huge amount of energy that we waste worrying about false beliefs.

Reflection

Reflection and self-examination are not works of a moment, they are an ongoing practice. There will be much more of both in the pages that follow and these are key Maverick skills. One way of improving a skill is to push out of your comfort zone.

Here are some advanced reflection questions that are designed to be hard. The first one is on the annual review form that I use with clients and always the one they find hardest. That is except for one client who for the first few years answered, 'Nothing!' Have a go, and it will be interesting at the end of the book to come back and update your answers. You will see a difference.

- What do you believe about yourself that limits you?

....

....

....

- What do others know that you do not know about yourself?

....

....

....

- What is a truth that you have never shared?

....

....

....

How does it feel to write that final truth down? What would be the next step; to share it with another? Or does an action come straight to mind?

Another key Maverick practice is writing and journaling. By now you have started to fill in the pages of this book or your notebook. Like writing a diary, this becomes a practice, a daily or weekly routine that I hope you will continue long after you have finished reading. By communicating our inner thoughts through writing or discussion, we are forcing ourselves to examine, order and tidy them. Left uncommunicated, these thoughts can spiral out of control, a tornado of anxiety and half-truths.

In Summary

My summary of this chapter…

1. ....

2. ....

3. ....

Key Points

1. Growth and change are not possible without self-enquiry.
2. We need others' input to increase our self-awareness.
3. We can hold ourselves back with our beliefs and stories. We let false truths dominate our thinking. These can be modified.

CHAPTER TWO

Key Moments and What They Tell You

Whenever I am having a first session with a new client, I ask them to tell me their story. At this point, many people will ask where they should start; I will answer something like, 'Start where it feels relevant to what you want to work on.' However, I find that even with this guidance, people rarely begin their story from an early enough point.

This isn't a problem, of course, as a coaching relationship provides plenty of scope for further exploration. I find their start point provides an interesting indicator of self-awareness; where someone chooses to start tells me something about how they see themselves. Many will pick the beginning of their professional careers – their 'work'. Others might start in their teenage years and a few will give a broad sweeping statement about their childhood. I have never heard a client start with their earliest memory, even though this is always illuminating when it arises in later conversations.

Inevitably, as their story and the coaching relationship progresses, we return to their childhood and their relationship with their parents. What happens in the first 12 years of our lives has a *huge* impact on who we are, as does our genetic make-up. We have almost no control over these factors and few memories may mean we need to consult with parents and siblings to piece together the patterns of our childhood.

The psychologist Sonja Lyubomirsky found that our happiness has a set point that we tend to return to. On average, 50 per cent of this set point is determined by our genes and upbringing; 10 per cent by our life circumstances (much less than we would imagine) and 40 per cent by how we chose to spend our time and think about the world, i.e. what we can control.

For me, much of my narrative – and the fragility that I carry as an adult – was shaped by a two-week period over Christmas 1981. I was eight years old and had been taken to the doctor with suspected epilepsy due to fits I was having. The doctor (thank you, Dr B) asked my mother what was going on at home as he suspected the fits were psychosomatic (a physical illness caused by a mental factor such as internal conflict or stress). My parents had been shouting a lot at each other; I remember the feeling of sitting at the top of the stairs listening to them late into the night.

My father was an alcoholic; he had tried, and then refused, to get treatment. My mother faced a dreadful decision, but the doctor made it easy: his opinion was that the fits were a clear sign that the environment had become toxic at home and that my siblings and I were no longer safe there. Damage was being done. Two days later, on 23 December, my mother drove up to the house in a different car and we drove away without my father.

The conversations were difficult, confusing and upsetting. They ended abruptly two weeks later when I was sent to boarding school for the first time and faced an enforced six weeks of no contact with my mother apart from writing letters. Because we had moved unexpectedly, I was enrolling four terms late, trying to join with well-established friendship groups and savvy boys who knew their way around the system. I was the only new boy and I was struggling. Three of my earliest memories come from this period:

- sitting on the stairs, hearing my parents shouting
- the shiny red car with orange kids' seatbelts and the strangeness as the front passenger seat remained empty

- chasing my mother's car down the street in my slippers on the first night at school.

So, what was going on for me and my story here? In the language of psychology, I had lost my only secure attachments; it was a severing that happened too early and without warning. Within the space of two weeks, I had been abandoned (so it seemed) by both my father and my mother. I don't blame my mother; she was suddenly a single parent with three kids under eight, and she made the best choices she could. For better or worse, though, this was the formation of 'little Ed' – the inner me who has been my tormentor and protector ever since.

I was forced to grow up instantly and that schism created a snapshot of my eight-year-old self that has remained stuck in time. I had to get on with it, I had to create a coat of armour. On one level this has given me a sense of independence and self-reliance that has served me well. On another, it created a fear of rejection, an emotional shut down and an insecurity that has hampered my happiness. This often happens around trauma. There is a dislocation that creates a split between the child you were before the event and the different, perhaps more separate and mature, child that the trauma created.

My work with clients has shown me that most of us have a version of little Ed inside us, many of us suffer one or more Adverse Childhood Experiences (e.g. emotional abuse or exposure to domestic violence) which profoundly shape our personalities and behaviour. One key way of helping ourselves and staying out of our own way involves befriending our little selves. Knowing this character and recognizing that our little selves are simply trying to protect us, to keep us safe, allows us to take a compassionate and encompassing view of this version of ourselves.

The little self can however be destructive and recognizing when they are hacking the system (normally when we behave in a way that surprises or disappoints us) makes it possible for us to remedy the hack before damage is done. We will explore this idea further in Chapter 11, when we look at relationships with ourselves and others (*see also* page 131). If you believe you have experienced one or more ACEs, there is some further reading suggested in the references section at the end of this book (*see also* page 250).

There are certain points in all our stories that are key moments, sometimes referred to as 'crucibles' as they tend to be transformational. This was one of mine and probably the most powerful environmental contributor to what makes me who I am today. That enforced severing of attachment, and the need to develop a coping strategy, has caused problems, but at some level the independence and self-sufficiency gained also enabled me to explore my own Maverick Path. Reflecting on our crucible moments gives us a better understanding of who we are and a chance to harness our Inner Maverick rather than be ruled by it.

So that's me: now it's time for you to tell your story. I am not with you to hear it, so rather than speak out loud to an empty room, I am asking you to draw it instead. The lifeline exercise below is a powerful one as it captures feelings and events in a single line.

Lifeline

Draw two axes of a chart. The x-axis, across the bottom, marks time, starting when you want to start, right up to the present. The vertical axis, the y-axis, marks a scale of fulfilment that you can intuit at this point. Don't overthink this; it doesn't need to be completely scientific, we just want a nice clear visual representation of how fulfilled, content or happy you were in life at any given moment.

Now, start to chart the progress of your life – start a line at the left and draw up and down as time moves on to the present. Label the key peaks and troughs of the line. I would recommend doing the first couple of versions in pencil. A generic example is shown opposite. Please make the events as specific as you can.

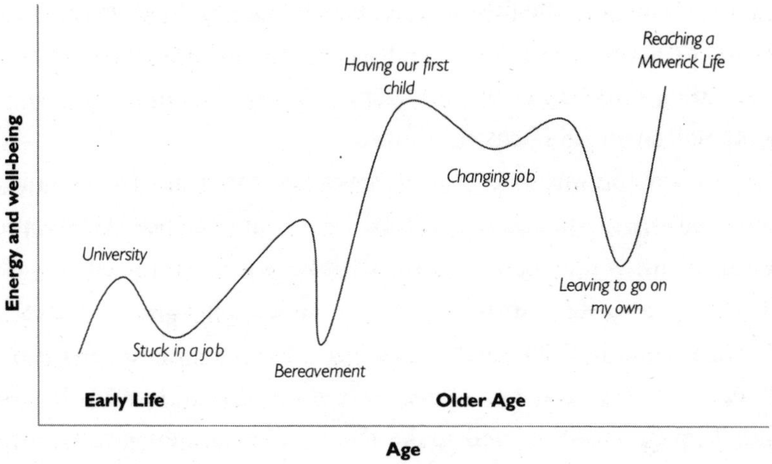

What does your line look like? A steady upward trend? It's more likely that you have ups and downs. Where is the line heading now? If you extended it out over the next five years, how does the trend look? What surprised you? Take a moment to look at some of the troughs and peaks; what led up to them?

We will return to this chart many times throughout the book.

We all have troughs, of course. How we deal with them has a large impact on our relationship with ourselves and with others. Trauma that is brushed under the carpet or happens before we have the vocabulary to process it always resurfaces. Our childhood knocks become our limiting beliefs that we carry around with us and these are the foundations of impostor syndrome. It is possible, though, to work through traumas; doing this work results in what is known as Post-traumatic Growth.

This is where we come to the concept of resilience, which is the ability to 'bounce back' from something that knocks you, or even 'bounce forward' to borrow a concept from the Harvard psychologist Dr Tal Ben-Shahar.

Looking back to the lifeline you drew, what was the direction of the line after the troughs? How quickly did the line start to move up again? Sometimes, in the moment, it is not clear how the challenges you are facing will shape and help your future.

Apple co-founder Steve Jobs talked about this in his famous commencement speech at Stanford University in 2005. He dropped out of his university course at Reed College after six months, which allowed him to start dropping in on courses that interested him. At the time Reed had an amazing calligraphy course and Jobs started attending these. Ten years later, when he was designing the first Mac, these courses helped make the first computer with beautiful fonts. He could not see at the time the importance of that calligraphy course, but in following what interested him, years later he could join the dots.

So, we become adults with a set of attachments and traumas. Often, we have not had the chance to sit with a therapist or counsellor to work through our feelings of hurt, failure or rejection, and these unprocessed feelings create a void in us, an empty space that most of us spend the rest of our lives trying to fill. Some try to fill the void with work. Others might use drugs, sex or alcohol. Other methods might be chasing adventure or a shedding/avoidance of responsibility. Some people have deep voids, others shallower, but we all have some feeling of emptiness or need for more. Subsequent events in our lives sometimes make the void worse, or sometimes help to fill it.

Tim grew up thinking he was not good enough. His void was created by a father continually undermining him and making him feel small and inadequate. He was gifted at maths and good at building relationships, so he went into finance. By the narrow metric of money, he was very successful. He set out to show his father and himself that he was good enough and conveniently there was a very clear and public scoring system – wealth. Our reflection on this was as follows: 'The void helps create the cash, but the cash can't fill the void'.

The Void

What might your void look like? This may be similar to one of the limiting beliefs or negative stories you identified in the last chapter (*see also* page 9). A hazy idea is fine at this point; we will return to the idea through the book. Note some thoughts down below.

....

....

....

....

Understanding your void allows you to start work on it. Recognizing some unhealthy tactics that you have subconsciously used in the past to try and fill the void means you can shift those tactics. Starting to work on it helps you become what the poet David Whyte beautifully refers to as the 'ancestor of your future happiness'.

In Summary

My summary of this chapter...

1. ....

2. ....

3. ....

Key Points

1. A small number of key moments have a large impact on your life.
2. Positive or negative; it is how we deal with the moment, rather than the moment itself, that determines our future happiness.
3. Left unexamined and unprocessed, negative life events will have a deleterious future effect.

CHAPTER THREE

What Matters to You?

Before the global COVID-19 pandemic, I would hear two types of response when I asked people what really mattered to them. I would either see a surprised look, followed by audible gears grinding in their head and steam coming out of their ears, or I'd receive a rather generic answer about kids and work. At the time of writing, the pandemic is not yet over. After two years of lockdowns, death tolls, overflowing hospitals, work and financial insecurity, a different kind of answer is emerging. Being deprived of what we consider fundamental to our existence provides a chance to reflect on what we really miss and what *really* matters to us. There is nothing good about a global pandemic, but perhaps one of the silver linings is an ability to become more discerning and careful in how, and on what, we choose to spend our limited time.

Values

Whatever has caused you to pick up this book, re-examining priorities is at the heart of living a Maverick Life. The drivers that determine what is important to us are our *values*. A value can be defined as the moral principle or accepted standards of a person or group. Our core values are somewhat hard coded from our early environment and experiences, although the hierarchy of importance can perhaps shift over time. They are part of the core software that we run, determining our behaviour and our choices, as well as how satisfied we are at any point in time. Values are the root answer to the question 'What is important to you?' Take money as an example. Often people say money is important to them, so the follow-up question is 'What is important to you about money?' This is called taking a Socratic approach – you keep digging deeper with each question.

For many, the eventual answer that *starts* with money ends with freedom. Money is important not in and of itself, but because it gives that person freedom or a sense of control. Alternatively, some people may say it gives a sense of winning or achievement. What's key is that both are true and valid because they are the true root – the value – that lies behind what is seemingly important (money). There are no right or wrong values. This isn't something to compare with other people or some idealized imaginary person, these are *your* values and knowing them is truly important.

Values

Have a think about what is important to you and apply the Socratic approach above. What do you defend, what upsets you, what makes you happy? All these moments give a clue as to a value that is either being honoured (happy) or challenged (upset). Think about why you were proud or fulfilled. What factors contributed to this? What did others do that helped you feel like this? Make a draft list of 10–20 values that you think you may have. If you're completely stuck, have a look at the list on the next page – you don't need to use this or stick to it, but it might give you an idea of where to start if you're struggling.

Once you have your longer list, look to see if some values are similar to each other and group those values. You might end up with four to six groups. If you have more, try to consolidate or remove the less-important groups. There is no right way of doing this, tune into what makes sense for you. These are your values and intensely personal. Group them in a way that makes sense to you, personally. Pick one value or create a word that summarizes each group. You now have your core values.

Sample List of Values

Accountability	Fairness	Popularity
Achievement	Faith	Power
Adventure	Fame	Proactive
Advocacy	Family	Professional
Ambition	Flexibility	Quality
Appreciation	Friendships	Recognition
Attractiveness	Fun	Religion
Authenticity	Growth	Reputation
Authority	Happiness	Resilience
Autonomy	Honesty	Resourcefulness
Balance	Humour	Respect
Beauty	Inclusiveness	Responsibility
Boldness	Independence	Responsiveness
Calmness	Influence	Risk taking
Challenge	Integrity	Security
Citizenship	Inner Harmony	Self-Respect
Collaboration	Justice	Service
Commitment	Kindness	Simplicity
Community	Knowledge	Spirituality
Competency	Leadership	Stability
Compassion	Learning	Status
Consistency	Love	Success
Contribution	Loyalty	Thoughtfulness
Courage	Meaningful	Trustworthiness
Creativity	Openness	Uniqueness
Curiosity	Optimism	Warmth
Determination	Passion	Wealth
Diversity	Patriotism	Well-being
Empathy	Peace	Wisdom
Equality	Pleasure	Work

Did you find that easy, or difficult? Don't worry if you found it challenging – most people do, especially if it's the first time they've tried the exercise. It can help to approach the question in a few different ways; for example, another source of information might be the lifeline you drew in Chapter 2 (*see also* page 17). Go back and study the peaks and troughs more closely. The troughs are likely to be times when your values are not being honoured, where you are not able to live by them. If family is a value then the estrangement or inaccessibility of a family member would be a trough and will confirm that value.

Peaks, on the other hand, are likely to be periods when you are living true to your values. If freedom is a value for you, then a peak might be travelling around the world, or a period between jobs, or when you started working for yourself. Really think about what was happening in those peak and trough moments and whether they added to or confirmed the list of values.

Friends and family are another good source of feedback on your values. Try the list out with them; you may get some surprises. Some of these values can be quite hidden, but the idea is that for a Maverick Life, you are openly and honestly living your values and choosing how you spend your time and energy according to them.

Values matter. If you set goals that do not fit with your values, you are very unlikely to achieve them. Likewise, relationships with others who have different core values to you can be difficult and complicated. Spending long periods in an environment or culture that does not mirror your values can be detrimental to your mental and physical health. The Maverick Path is one of gradual transition though, having a plan and moving towards that plan minimizes the risk and stress for you and makes it easier to be in an environment that you find challenging.

Values Ranked

Now, for the final piece of the puzzle, you are going to have a go at ranking your values. To do this, take two of these values and ask yourself which one you could not live without. Repeat this with each value – for example, a set of values could be integrity, kindness, achievement, family and fairness. Would you rather have integrity over achievement? If yes, then this places the integrity value above the achievement value. Now ask yourself whether you would rather have family over achievement? If yes, then family goes above achievement. Integrity or family? If integrity, then that stays at the top followed by family and then achievement. Post-it notes are a great help here. You will end up with a ranked list of values that might look like this:

1. Integrity
2. Family
3. Kindness
4. Fairness
5. Achievement.

Write your values here

1. ....

2. ....

3. ....

4. ....

5. ....

Recognizing our core values is important because when we need to choose or decide something, we can do so easily by determining if the choice lines up with our true values. Think about behaviours that allow you to show and build your values and those that do not. This is also a good moment to share your list with a partner or a friend – they can help point out when you are living your values and when you are not. Over time you will be able to identify that queasy feeling that accompanies a bending of one of your values and that complete feeling that accompanies true living of a value.

Key Relationships

We have talked about what matters to you, so how about *who* matters to you? In his book *The Tipping Point*, Malcolm Gladwell presents Dunbar's number. The theory shows that the brain can maintain social relationships with a limited number of people. The number is 150. It is often the size of early hunter-gatherer clans, eleventh-century churches, modern factories and Christmas card lists.

It is no coincidence that parties also seem to hover at around 70–150 people. While the 150 is important, the inner circle is more so. This is a group of friends, family and perhaps colleagues who really matter to you – it's going to be a number much smaller than 150.

Robin Dunbar is a British evolutionary psychologist whose work showed that humans can maintain around 15 very close friendships, 50 close friendships and 150 friends. This has a real impact on how we choose to spend our time and which relationships we focus on.

My Circles

Draw a small circle with you in the middle of a page, then add circles around it for each group of people that matters, e.g. friends, family, colleagues.

Now, around each of these circles, write the names of the people that really count for that circle. Think of being shipwrecked and put in a lifeboat. Who would you really like to have in the boat with you? We would not just choose those who can steer a boat, but also those who could keep us cheerful, help us eat and manage to get on with others on board.

This is your constellation. An example is below:

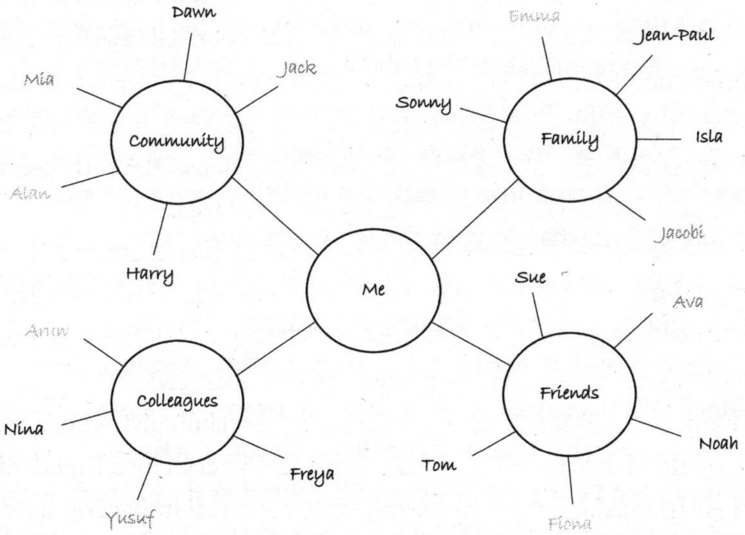

What do you notice? Was this an easy exercise, or did you have to really think about it? Are there dozens of names on the page or just a few? Are they spread across the different circles or very concentrated on one area?

Now, take a different colour pen and highlight the relationships that are in good shape. With a third colour, highlight those that need some work. Don't overthink this, just highlight those people you are naturally drawn to, both positively and negatively.

Who would you like to see more of and who drains too much from you? Add a little plus or minus on the constellation by these people. What does the balance look like?

We will return to this constellation in the later sections of the book, but for now, take a moment to reflect on what you see and what comes up for you.

Passions

We have covered core values and the important people in your life. Now let's think about the interests and activities that have soul for you. What do you read? What YouTube videos or podcasts are you drawn to? We will cover the difference between a hobby and a job later on, but for now, what are the areas of life and work that you get excited about? What do you love to talk about? When you meet people you find interesting, what do your conversations consist of?

This is the start of looking at your soul – what you are passionate about. Our passions are sometimes hidden, obscured by layers of expectations and a work ethic that we mysteriously inherited or assumed. We think that work is separate from our passions. You can probably guess what I think about that – the Maverick works with their passions – but before we can properly answer that assertion, we need to reconnect with our souls and figure out what really fires us up. What makes your heart beat faster or slower?

Another way to help you figure this out is to think about the causes that pull your heartstrings or where you choose to donate time or money. These are often apparent from an early age. What would you write a book about or what would your 10-minute TED Talk be about?

Passions

Make a list of activities and areas that have real draw and meaning for you. Some may be obvious, a sport like golf or tennis, others more subtle, like walking along the coast, meaningful conversations with friends or mentoring others. Come back to this and ask others for input.

. . . .

. . . .

. . . .

Now think about how you spend your time: how much time do you spend on the list above? Is your work on these passions paid or unpaid? Would you like to spend more time on the things on the list? The answer is likely yes, so what will you spend less time on to make space for them?

One of my colleagues shared this incredibly simple idea from their mother, who was a neurosurgeon. Her theory was to spend more time on the things that you enjoy and that bring you pleasure and less time on those that do not. A simple idea, but in reality, we spend much of our lives working against this principle. We are experts at convincing ourselves that we must work hard, to mortgage our current happiness for some future date that we may never see. What might happen if we followed through and reorganized our time around our passions?

Time Goals

Make your list; what would you like to spend more and less time on?

Five things I would like to spend more time doing:

....

....

....

....

....

Five things I would like to spend less time doing:

....

....

....

....

....

If you had total freedom, financially, from responsibilities and psychological limitations, what would you choose to spend your time doing? This is a mind-boggling question for many of us.

Finish this sentence in your own words:

If I had total freedom I would...

....

....

....

At this point, it may start to feel like this is a pipe dream. It may feel unrealistic and out of reach – but stay with me. The Maverick will give an answer to these questions that is close to what they are currently doing. That is what it means to design your life with a real understanding of what is important to you. To live in a Maverick way.

Simon Mottram trained as an accountant and was working in a marketing agency. He was passionate about two things: cycling and fashion. He felt that cycling clothing was plain, uninspiring and not fit for purpose. His passion for cycling was about the positive impact on health and relationships that he experienced. He wanted to share this and so he set out with a bold mission to make cycling the most popular sport in the world. Clothing was his way of carrying out that mission and so he did this through clothing, story-telling and engaging experiences at the company he set up: Rapha.

In Summary

My summary of this chapter...

1. ....

2. ....

3. ....

Key Points

1. Your values are fixed early in life and are your operating system – they really matter.
2. They determine what and who you will enjoy spending time on.
3. Once you understand this, you can intentionally design how you spend your time.

CHAPTER FOUR

The LQ Self-Discovery Scale

Now that we have considered our passions and values, and started being honest with ourselves, this chapter aims to help you take a snapshot of your life as a whole. This picture of your life at a moment in time can act as a baseline from which you can start to identify areas to work on. Some areas you may already be aware of and this chapter will help confirm your suspicions, but others may be a surprise to you – as such, it can be a useful diagnostic tool. As part of this, we will look at how well balanced or in harmony your life is. Too much work? Not enough exercise or time with others? You may be aware of this as a sort of creeping unease, but here we aim to shine a spotlight on it.

In many countries we take our cars in for an annual check-up and service. This helps keep cars safe, emissions down and makes sure vehicles are fit to be on the roads. Being used to this as a principle, it is strange that we do not put ourselves in for an annual check-up in the same way – this is what the Life Quotient (LQ) tool is designed to do. There are 12 parts to this tool, covering life areas such as sleep, occupation and your life partner. Instead of road-worthiness, we're looking at our life-worthiness. These are the underlying pillars that, when in good shape and combined with a clear purpose, can lead you to a more fulfilled life.

A high LQ score means you are Life Fit, which is the underpinning of a Maverick Life. It shows that you have attended to all areas of your life and that there is relative harmony. It also shows that your mind and body are operating at a positive level, providing you with the energy to pursue your best life. These pillars have been developed and tested during my reading and coaching over the last 20 years.

The first four pillars are grouped under the area of self. Often we forget to start with the self. Without it though we can struggle to be in relationship to others or effective in our chosen work. Both mind and body are covered. They are deeply interconnected, we all know the phrase 'healthy body, healthy mind'. To live a Maverick Life we need both physical and mental resources. A calm mind. A rested body (sleep) that is well fuelled (nutrition) and strong (exercise).

The second area is other people. We have evolved to live in groups and support each other. Dan Gilbert the American psychologist wrote: 'If I wanted to know about your happiness, and I could know only one thing about you, I wouldn't want to know your gender, religion health or income. I'd want to know about your social network – about your friends and family and the strength of your bonds with them.'

The third area is work – what we choose to do with the majority of our time. This may be paid work or it could be unpaid through volunteering or caring for children, for example. Our sense of purpose is closely tied to our work and without work that fulfils us, it is hard to be invested and living a life we believe in.

When we have these three areas in balance with each other, and the pillars are relatively well developed, then we experience a surge in energy and intent. Combine that with a clear view of purpose and we start to have major impact in a focused way that the world desperately needs right now.

Development in each of these pillars is both essential and a lifelong endeavour; don't feel discouraged if you feel like you have lots of work to do – that's the point.

LQ Exercise

As a quick starter, give each of the 12 pillars a score out of 10, based on how that area is in your life right now, with 10 being great and 1 being poor. If you do not have one of the pillars currently in your life, then score how happy you are with that situation. A low score would indicate that you would like to make a change.

LQ Pillar	Score out of 10
Self	
1. State of mind	
2. Sleep	
3. Eating and drinking	
4. Exercise	
Others	
5. Partner	
6. Kids	
7. Friends and family	
8. Community and planet	
Work	
9. Occupation	
10. Giving	
11. Learning	
12. Productivity	

What do you notice about your scores already?

There are two ways to take the full test. I recommend you go online and create an account at The Modern Maverick website (www.themodernmaverick.com). This gives you access to the full test which will be easier to complete digitally. If you need a code you can email us on team@themodernmaverick.com

If you prefer the old-school method, you can use a pen and paper on the printed version of the test, which is below. If you do not currently have one of the pillars (partner or kids), answer the first question in the pillar and then use that score as your average for that pillar: 1 means you strongly disagree, you do not see yourself like this; 10 is strongly agree and you recognize yourself in the statement.

LQ diagnostic			**Score out of 10**
Self			
	1) State of Mind		
		i. I like myself	
		ii. I have a manageable level of stress and anxiety in my life	
		iii. I am clear on my strengths and I put them to good use	
		iv. My inner voice is not too loud and is broadly helpful	
		v. I keep my emotions under control and interact with others in a way that I am happy with	
	Total for state of mind		
	Average for state of mind (divide by 5)		
	2) Sleep		
		i. I fall asleep easily and sleep through the night	
		ii. I wake feeling rested and have good energy levels	
		iii. I generally get as much sleep as a I need	
		iv. I am good at taking breaks during the day	
		v. I regularly take holidays and switch off during these breaks	
	Total for sleep		
	Average for sleep (divide by 5)		
	3) Eating and drinking		
		i. I eat a well balanced diet	
		ii. Most of what I eat is freshly prepared	

		iii. I am near the weight I would like to be	
		iv. I have a healthly relationship with food	
		v. I am happy with the amount of alcohol I drink	
	Total for eating and drinking		
	Average for eating and drinking (divide by 5)		
	4) Exercise		
		i. I can do everything physically that I want to	
		ii. I exercise at least three times per week for half an hour or more	
		iii. I enjoy the exercise I do	
		iv. I set myself exercise goals	
		v. I am pain free	
	Total for exercise		
	Average for exercise (divide by 5)		
Total for Self (add the totals from the four pillars above)			
Average for self (divide by 20)			
Others			
	1) Partner		
		i. If I have a partner our relationship is positive, if I do not have a partner I am happy with that	
		ii. We communicate openly and regularly and we share our vulnerabilities	
		iii. I feel safe and trust my partner	
		iv. There is mutual respect in place	
		v. I feel seen and supported by my partner	
	Total for partner		
	Average for partner (divide by 5 if all questions anwered or by 1 if only i. answered)		
	2) Kids		
		i. If I have kids our relationship is positive, if I do not have children I am happy with that	
		ii. My kids are generally flourishing	
		iii. If they are school age they enjoy school	
		iv. I am able to communicate with them openly and honestly, they talk to me about their problems	

		v. I prioritize them above all else and spend enough time with them	
	Total for kids		
	Average for kids (divide by 5 if all questions anwered or by 1 if only i. answered)		
	3) Friends and Family		
		i. On the whole my relationships with my family are good	
		ii. I have enough friends, new and old	
		iii. I see my friends and family as much as I would like	
		iv. When I see my friends and family it is fun	
		v. I have a handful of people I could call on if I needed to	
	Total for friends and family		
	Average for friends and family (divide by 5)		
	4) Community and planet		
		i. I have a clear sense of my local community and feel like I belong	
		ii. I am involved in my local community at the level I would like to be	
		iii. I am making a positive impact on the world	
		iv. I understand and am engaged with climate change	
		v. I have a clear plan that I am acting on for how I can help with the climate crisis	
	Total for community and planet		
	Average for community and planet (divide by 5)		
Total for Others (add the totals for the four pillars above)			
Average for others (divide by 20)			
Work			
	1) Occupation		
		i. I am clear on my purpose and my life is in line with this purpose	
		ii. I have enough money	
		iii. I have a good balance in my life, my amount of work is about right	

		iv. I am clear on my own definition of success and work towards this	
		v. I feel able to contribute in the work I do and that contribution is recognised and valued	
	Total for occupation		
	Average for occupation (divide by 5)		
	2) Giving		
		i. I am happy with the time I give to others	
		ii. I have a clear giving plan for money and I give enough	
		iii. I show up for my friends and family	
		iv. People would consider me generous	
		v. I use my network to increase my impact	
	Total for giving		
	Average for giving (divide by 5)		
	3) Learning		
		i. I feel like I am still learning as much as I would like to	
		ii. I have enough fun and novelty in my life	
		iii. I have hobbies that I enjoy and spend enough time on	
		iv. I am clear on what I would like to learn next	
		v. I am learning and developing at work	
	Total for learning		
	Average for learning (divide by 5)		
	4) Productivity		
		i. I am efficient and productive, I get done what I need to get done	
		ii. I am happy with the amount of time I spend consuming news and other media	
		iii. I rarely feel overwhelmed	
		iv. I am happy with my use of social media and other digital communication channels	
		v. I have a healthy relationship with technology	
	Total for productivity		
	Average for productivity (divide by 5)		

Total for work (add the totals from the four pillars above)		
Average for work (divide by 20)		
Summary Table		
	Average score for Self	
	Average score for Others	
	Average score for Work	
Total LQ (add the totals from all 12 pillars above)		
Average score (divide by 60)		

You will receive (or generate) an average score for each of the 12 pillars. First, take a look at how these detailed scores compare with your first pass earlier in the chapter (*see also* page 35). Next, for the lower scores that you would like to work on, find the questions that scored lowest within those pillars. Start to jot down some ideas about how you could improve those scores. We cover each of these pillars in Part III of the book so for now, put your jottings aside – we will return to them in more detail later in the book.

Everyone scores differently; for some a 9 would be unheard of, while for others anything below a 7 is a disaster. This makes it hard to comment on your overall score. Broadly, anything around 500 and above is a strong LQ score. If you find yourself below 300 then taking action and perhaps seeking help from a coach or other professional is key.

Pippa knew something wasn't right. Tired all the time and perpetually overwhelmed, she was getting through her days and weeks, time was flying but also dragging at the same time. She took the LQ test and her first observation was that she spent nearly 75 per cent of her time on work and all the pillars in work were low-scoring. She also found that her scores for exercise, sleep and others were all low.

During COVID she had become particularly focused on work, blurring boundaries between self and work. She had fallen out of the habit of nurturing and spending time on her relationships and so she created four slots in each week where she would leave home to exercise or to see others. The first two weeks were hard, but then gradually a pattern emerged and a routine was established. As she began to feel more energy and support from others, she was able to take a look at her work. She decided to stay but on different terms.

In Summary

My summary of this chapter…

1. ....

2. ....

3. ....

Key Points

1. It is useful to assess where you are currently on a set of key life pillars.
2. For a happy, healthy life, there needs to be a balance and good scores across the three areas and 12 pillars: this is Life Fit.
3. A low overall score indicates the need for major change or revolution, while individual low scores show areas for evolution.

PART II

Dream

CHAPTER FIVE

You're Not in the Spotlight

Know this: no one else is watching the movie of your life. Maybe you knew this already, or perhaps this feels radical to you – but just think about it. How many movies do you watch of other people's lives? How many people are you truly scrutinizing in the way that you sometimes fear others are scrutinizing you? I'm willing to bet that although you are interested in other people, that you care for them and you try to help, you're not watching in all that much detail.

Take someone close to you: maybe a child, a partner or a parent. Their movie runs 24 hours a day, seven days a week for roughly 80 years. That is 700,000 hours. How many of those hours do you feature in the film? Even if you are married for 50 years and sleep in the same bed, you might make it up to 200,000 hours. If you do not live with them, then maybe 2,000 hours over 80 years. How many hours, when you are not with that person, are you thinking about them, imagining what they are doing and thinking? Maybe double the 2,000 hours to 4,000 hours?

Yes, others care about us, but in a global way, not the detail of what we do with our lives. The truth is, in the nicest possible sense, no one else gives a s***. We become too caught up thinking about what others would think. We worry about what we should do. We hold on tight to a version of ourselves that we think is expected. What others really want is to know that we are happy if they are fond of us or that we are sad if we are their enemy.

Even parents or lovers have more than enough in front of them, trying to figure their own way through life without worrying endlessly about you. And this is when we are talking about people who know you and love you. What about people who have spent zero hours in your film? Or those tangential characters – the followers on Instagram, for example, who have spent mere seconds in a hyper-edited semi-fictional account of your life movie. Do they count?

This truth, if you let it, can be deeply liberating. Think how much time we all spend worrying about our audience, or trying to please a parent, or bending ourselves to the wills of society. Once we accept that we are on our own, far from creating loneliness, it can free us up to take our Maverick Path, to really figure out what makes us tick. In doing so, we end up making a far more interesting and 'successful' movie anyway, even if there *were* people watching – which there aren't.

So who are you making your movie for? An abstract sense of society at large – what should I do, what is expected of me, how do I fit in?

Then there are people in our lives who exert a strong influence over what we choose to do. I work with clients who are often second-guessing what key people in their lives would wish them to do. Rarely do they check in with these people; if they did, the answers might be surprising. The most obvious example I see is around living up to perceived paternal expectations. Our parents, and particularly our fathers, seem to have an almost gravitational influence on key decisions and the direction we take. We worry about their judgements, but these say more about the weaknesses they have than the problems they think we may be facing.

James came to me in the middle of his career, successful in the non-Maverick sense, but totally stuck and trapped. In the second session he began to talk about a career he wished he had in Architecture. Then he lit up as he told me about some clay he had recently bought to start ceramics again after a 30-year gap. I asked him what had led him into his current career and he started to talk about his father, grandfather and other ancestors. He felt an enormous pressure to conform and to succeed on their metrics, which were very financial and profile-based. The irony of course is that in borrowing someone else's definition of success James hadn't really smashed it and fulfilled his own potential. He wasn't passionate about what he was doing; he wasn't uniquely talented in it. We talked about how he was working with one hand tied behind his back. He had worked very hard to do well and to please his ancestors, but such efforts came at a great cost to himself.

We rehearsed a difficult and overdue conversation with his father, where James let his dad know that he was OK, grateful for his input and that over the next few months and years he was going to transition into work that was more creative and architecture-led. In the end he gave his dad a big hug, thanked him and with that, he was free.

Key Influencers

Turn back to your constellation on page 27. Now, make a list of people who have a strong influence on your decision making. This might be one person or a group of people. You may know them well or they could be an abstract group, e.g. society as a whole. Note what you do to try and please them and how they have shaped the course of your life. If you can, go and talk to them about this, asking open questions and checking in with them.

Person/Group 1

....

Areas of influence

....

....

Person/Group 2

....

Areas of influence

....

....

Person/Group 3

....

Areas of influence

....

....

Of course, it's not just worrying about what others might see. The idea of scrutiny is compounded by the dangers of comparison – even if you're not concerned about what people might think of you, perhaps you are silently worrying about how you look or perform or achieve up against someone you admire. But it's the same trap, in a different guise – comparison does not help you live a free life. As the mother of a client used to say to her, 'Stop comparing your insides to someone else's outsides.'

Social media has turbocharged this insidious game of comparison and instead of liberating us, it ties us to these misperceptions of what 'good' looks like. Money, medals and mentions become the driver of our thoughts and behaviours, but for many these are the wrong measures and are likely to be at best inflated and at worst made up.

We compound this by creating hybrid super people, where we take the best aspect of several others and combine them into some hyper being that we then compare ourselves to. If only I could have A's brains with B's body, C's hair and, oh yes please, D's job and E's comic timing. Maybe throw in F's memory and G's house by the sea. How about H's well-behaved dog and I's bank account? And so on.

But no one is this super being and no one is as calm or successful on the inside as they might project on the outside. Much like a swan, they may appear to be gliding across the surface but underneath their legs are paddling like crazy. Outwardly successful, inwardly miserable.

We can also do the opposite. Comparing ourselves to those that we perceive to be below us, doing less well. This creates a false sense of smugness and again is rarely based on the truth.

Nothing is as it seems. I remember sitting behind the perfect-looking family on a flight: four beautiful children and a handsome couple. She was a row behind the others and journaling. As I walked past her in the aisle, two sentences scrawled in huge bold capital letters leapt off the page:

> I CANNOT GO ON
> WHEN WILL HE RESPECT ME?

It was a wake-up call for me, focus on my path and stop making judgements or comparisons that in the end only hold me back. We grow up celebrating external or extrinsic measures of success. Externally, we look for a sense of validation, a sense of self – exam results, sporting results, competitions won. We rely on the applause of others and the grading system of others for our sense of self-worth. Many of us are encouraged to go to university for further baptism by examiners and then roll off the production line into our first jobs, still looking outwards for our signals of success. Not only are the measures wrong, but the *source* of the scores is wrong too.

What about looking inside ourselves? How do we feel? How do we start to internally validate ourselves? What matters to us? The Maverick marks their own exam papers, sets their own questions and works on

areas that need improving on their own time and inclination, not based on the aspirations of others.

Comparison Points

Who do you compare yourself to, favourably and unfavourably? Siblings often feature here – we have grown up naturally in competition with them, imagining our parents comparing us.

Person 1

....

Comparison Points

....

....

Person 2

....

Comparison Points

....

....

Person 3

....

Comparison Points

....

....

Write down what conclusions you draw from the comparisons. Do you do a lot of comparing? Do you tend to compare favourably or unfavourably? Up or down? Are you basing these comparisons on facts or perceptions? Remember the Court of Law exercise (*see also* page 8)? Try running some of your comparisons through that process. Do they stand up? How do these conclusions help you? The less we compare the easier it is for us to focus on our own versions of what matters and to create our own internal sense of satisfaction.

A headmaster said to one of the parents: 'We help our pupils be first-class versions of themselves, not a second-class version of someone else.' How can you help yourself to be a first-class version of you?

In Summary

My summary of this chapter…

1. ....

2. ....

3. ....

Key Points

1. We spend too much time worrying about what others think and comparing ourselves to false impressions of others.
2. The Maverick looks for internal measures of success rather than relying on external validation.
3. Other people have more than enough of their own stuff to worry about.

CHAPTER SIX

Defining Your Own Version of Success

Whenever I hear that phrase, usually spoken in slightly hushed tones – 'Oh yes, they're doing really well, they've been really successful' – I have two reactions. The first is the initial, human, kneejerk response – for me, it's either mild jealousy or joy for the person concerned, depending on my own state of mind. Then, I stop and wonder what the speaker means by this statement. What is the metric for 'doing well'? How is this observer judging what 'successful' means?

Of course, some immediate ideas spring to mind:

1) Money in the bank
2) Title and size of company
3) Number of Twitter followers
4) Column inches devoted to the individual
5) Number of employees in charge of
6) Size of house(s)
7) Sale of company they started.

You'll notice, though, that these are all external measures, both quantifiable and definable. They are also the result of many possible sacrifices. It is impossible to know what that person has had to do to achieve these seemingly important outcomes. The *real* questions I want to ask when I hear someone being described in this way is 'OK, but how *happy* are they, how fulfilled are they?'

On the one hand, this is a harder question to answer: you need to know the person, spend time with them and have honest and challenging conversations over a period of time with them. On the other hand, there are tests and surveys and if you really ask someone – I mean *truly* ask them – you may end up close to the real answer.

Happiness is an internal measure, not something that can be neatly judged by the outside eye. However, there may be some visible clues which may lead to a more Maverick definition of 'doing well':

1) Being in at least one committed, loving relationship (not necessarily a romantic one)
2) Liking what they do for work
3) Being in service of others
4) Having a group of close friends and seeing them regularly
5) Having energy
6) Maintaining meaningful relationships with children if they have them
7) No dependence on harmful substances
8) Fit and healthy
9) Anxiety-free
10) Calm, with limited anger
11) Finding flow through their work or hobbies
12) Speaking with passion about areas of their lives.

On some level, we all want to be successful. It is a basic human instinct. However, we spend little time thinking about what that means for us or how we calibrate this. Where do ideas of success come from?

Let's deconstruct this a little. How are our views of 'success' generally formed? There are strong forces that quietly and continually assert their influence over us, often without us consciously waking up to this.

Our parents give us our genes and those who bring us up give us our first framework for success. What is talked about around the dinner table? What did your caregivers' model in terms of work and the rewards for work, and what is important in life? Then we enter education, where almost immediately we have a peer group to compare to and figures of authority (teachers) who judge us and grade us. There is an unquestioned assumption that a B is better than a C and that effort is imperative. At no time in our lives are we so closely monitored or reported on. Next stop is our occupation. How much thought do we give to the success metrics for our work? There are very likely to be some Key Performance Metrics or KPIs, regardless of the specific role. They will look extremely different depending on whether you are working for a bank (likely to be financial) or a school (likely to be educational progress).

The danger is that if these are not aligned with our own metrics, then we can be coerced into adopting our work metrics. If we're not careful, what matters to our managers can come to dominate our viewpoints and feelings about ourselves and others. The Maverick is not defined solely by their work and not by what matters to our managers.

Our views are also shaped by the media that we consume. Depending on which echo chamber we find ourselves in, our biases can become magnified. The news celebrates sporting and business success stories, as well as reporting on extreme disasters and tragedies. Where is everything in the middle? In other words, where is 'real life'?

Hollywood presents us with a fantasy world. Social media algorithms select for outrage and bombard us with a curated set of semi-falsehoods. It is no wonder that money, medals and glitter are what we crave. Then, too, our economies and the governments that regulate them play a huge part in how we define success.

The stock market score is reported many times per day, despite only 33 per cent of people in the UK and 56 per cent in the US owning shares. Our governments measure success predominantly by GDP (Gross Domestic Product), which measures how much we make as a nation in terms of goods and money. There are alternatives to this metric for social success; Bhutan, for example, has GNH (Gross National Happiness), which can be seen as a measure of economic and moral progress. The GNH includes nine domains which give us clues as to how another system might work:

1) Psychological well-being
2) Health
3) Education
4) Time use
5) Cultural diversity and resilience
6) Good governance
7) Community vitality
8) Ecological diversity and resilience
9) Living standards.

Imagine how different the world would look if other countries had joined Bhutan in selecting GNH in the 1970s as their central measure of success.

Finally, our peers are a huge source of influence over what we choose to measure. They form a large part of our ecosystem and create a strong pull to compare ourselves to. Our in-group will have a set of values and ethics that we will be influenced by.

What Shapes My Understanding of Success?

Take a moment to write down what each of those forces means for you – don't overthink it, a few notes will do. The point is just to reflect on how these areas influence your thinking, for good or bad. Check your key influencers list from the previous chapter (page 47).

1. Parents and early environment

....

....

....

2. Education

....

....

....

3. Work

....

....

....

4. Media

....

....

....

5. Government and Economy

....

....

....

6. Peers

....

....

....

This morning I found myself on my LinkedIn feed. I don't have a big LinkedIn habit; for me, the platform tends to be a back door into social media as I'm not active on Facebook, Twitter or Instagram. Someone I once knew was announcing her new role as chair of an industry body. This is someone who I had not thought about for at least 10 years, being appointed to a body that I have no desire to get involved with, for various reasons… but still, I felt knocked a bit.

As I made the mistake of scrolling down further, more of my network's self-promotion nibbled away at me. I so wanted to be delighted for her, and for every other achievement I saw on my feed, but the inner critic jumped in, making unhelpful comparisons and leaving me feeling not good enough. These forces are real; my mood dipped significantly, even though I am aware of all this.

Comparison and societal definitions of success, whether you reject them or not, can make it hard to figure out our *own* definition of success and even harder to embark on making that success real. I'm not immune to this and I'm literally writing the book on it. Be kind to yourself and know that this is a battle everyone fights.

It's a mirage; the idea that by achieving some of the external versions of success, we will be happy. We all know the old chestnut about money not buying happiness – well, beyond meeting the basic needs of food, shelter and security, it's a cliché because it's true. But it's an attractive mirage and it's not surprising that we fall for it. We are driven to explore, always moving towards the new; this evolutionary impulse used to help us when we were hunting for food or looking for a mate. In today's world, though, it can lead to a sense of fleeting satisfaction alongside a sense of constantly seeking fulfilment.

Psychologists refer to this as the hedonic treadmill, which is also known as hedonic adaptation. We quickly seem to return to a set level of happiness despite major positive or negative events or life changes. Whether we win the lottery or have a major disabling accident, within a period of 12–24 months the research shows that, happiness-wise, we are broadly back to where we began. This suggests that attempts to bolster our well-being through external factors may be futile.

Other inbuilt drivers push us towards working hard on a narrow definition of success. We want to achieve, to feel like we are making a difference or impact. Increasingly, we want instant gratification, to find shortcuts. Working hard is idolized, particularly in the US where being busy is equated with success and importance. Finally, we crave certainty and a sense of control. All of these drivers can push us to work too hard towards a definition of success that is borrowed from others' expectations of us.

So now that we have covered all the ways *not* to define success, where might we look for a wiser version of it? A useful starting point might be talking to people at the end of their lives. This is what Bronnie Ware did for a living. She is a terminal care nurse who spent several years caring for people in the last weeks of their lives. In her book, *The Top Five Regrets of the Dying*, she writes that she heard many confessions of regret, which she summarized into five key phrases:

1) I wish I'd had the courage to live a life true to myself, not the life others expected of me
2) I wish I hadn't worked so hard
3) I wish I'd had the courage to express my feelings
4) I wish I'd stayed in touch with my friends
5) I wish that I'd let myself be happier.

Dying Regrets: A Chance to Reflect

How does this list make you feel? Clients have found it extremely powerful. Write down three reflections you have from reading the list:

1. ....

2. ....

3. ....

Mike came to me to reassess his life. He felt unhappy and that he was not fulfilling his potential. He lived in the US and he felt a strong focus on success at work, where he felt left behind by his peers. We looked at all areas of his life – he had a strong marriage and great relationships with his kids. He was an active part of the local community and was very fit and healthy.

When I pointed out that many areas of his life were in great shape, Mike dismissed this and said that work was more important. We talked about this; I shared the regrets of the dying with him. We looked at his definition of success and what was important to him. He saw that, without thinking, he had prioritized areas other than work – he felt this was just something he did anyway and that it was not important. His perspective began to shift, to place more weight and recognition on the non-work aspects of his life. He left our third session with a real bounce in his step. Work he could change, the harder things to change like his relationships were in great shape, thanks to the focus he had already placed there.

Another clue to where success and happiness lies comes from the longest-running psychological study in the world – The Grant Study, also known as the Harvard Study of Adult Development. Researchers set out to answer the key question of 'What makes a good life?'

The study started in 1938 with 268 men (Harvard sophomores – second-year students) and aimed to follow them through their lives, each year asking a series of questions and taking key measurements. In 1967, a further 456 disadvantaged youths were added to the study. There are three key takeaways:

1) Success is long term – look over the arc of a life. There is no point in dipping in and out of people's lives; a long-term view is needed. And in decision making the long-term view is the key one: what impact will this have on my life in five to 10 years' time?

2) Emotional Intelligence matters. Life is going to be full of triumphs and setbacks and it is the ability to adapt and move forward that matters.
3) It really is all about relationships. The study found a strong correlation between flourishing lives and their relationships with family, friends and communities. Robert Waldinger, the current director of the study, states: 'The people who were the most satisfied in their relationships at age 50 were the healthiest at age 80. Strong relationships help to delay mental and physical decline.'

The Book Within the Book Case Study

Setting out to write a book requires a great deal of self-motivation. That anxious inner monologue is on overdrive in any author's head. Who will read it? Who am I to think I can write a book? When will I have the time? Does the world even need another book? Writing this book has been a strong test of my Maverick Path. Paralysed by a fear of failure and judgement, it took me a long time to own it, to own up to it and to commit. I was frightened of the inevitable question: 'Who is your publisher?' To me, this felt like the ultimate non-Maverick question. I saw it as effectively asking if the book had been vetted by the 'experts' – is it bona fide? Is it a success in 'old metrics'? All of this speaks to an extrinsic model of the world, as we saw earlier (page 49). This would define the book's success along the lines of:

- Have I heard of your publisher?
- Did you get a big advance?
- How big is your existing audience?
- How many copies did you sell?

Thinking this way meant that for the first four years, this book went nowhere: it didn't even really get off the starting blocks because I was too afraid of not measuring up. Every little setback became a delay of weeks or months. Someone convinced me I could not write unless I had a profile to make the book attractive to publishers and my ego wanted a profile and a place in the world, while my head and heart were not so sure. With that lack of alignment, no wonder the book was going nowhere. Others asked why I even wanted to write a book. Why risk putting my head above the parapet when I was a private person and seemed to have a pretty good life?

So how did I break the cycle? I went 'conscious' on the problem. Instead of letting my subconscious play the normal tape of my learnt behaviours and engrained anxieties, I let the power of my engaged conscious mind loose. As we have already started to do for ourselves earlier in this chapter, I asked myself what a different set of success metrics might look like. I also worked with a fantastic book coach, who you can find in the reference section (*see also* page 251).

An alternative definition of success might perhaps mean writing for a smaller audience, recognizing that if five people have read and taken something from the book, then that is a positive impact on the world. Or maybe it could be writing to refine my thinking and my ability to communicate ideas to others. What about writing to develop the skill of writing, of overcoming the block? Framed like this, completing a chapter becomes a major achievement.

Discovering new publishing models where smaller print runs were possible further reduced writer's block. When my idea of a successful book moved from feeding off an external recognition of sales, likes and feedback to an internal need to organize my thoughts, develop my voice and send my message out into the world; when I went from desiring a bestseller to aiming to help 1,000 people in some small way that was the moment the pen filled with ink and the words started to flow.

Ben Hunt-Davis is an Olympic gold medallist in rowing. He and his business partner Tom Barry now run a flourishing coaching company called Will it Make the Boat Go Faster? One of their key mantras is to focus on the performance and the results will follow. The idea is not to chase results without having done the training or made the changes needed to the process. By making my goal *writing* the book, rather than the *sales* of the book, it freed up the process and my creativity so that the words started coming and the pages filled.

You are reading this book and as you will see from the spine, I did indeed find a publisher. I cannot pretend that it wasn't a great moment when someone agreed to publish it. Deep down, little Ed was chuffed to bits. I wish I was totally free from that piece of external validation; I don't think we ever quite rid ourselves of it, but by being aware we can understand clearly when it is hindering us. I was blocked by making the goal 'finding a publisher' rather than helping others. But the publishing offer did make me excited that more people might read the book and that it might reach a larger audience.

One Goal We All Need to Include in our Definition of Success

Your definition of success is deeply personal and bespoke. Are there some aspects of success though that might be universal? I would like to offer one that I really believe we all need to include. No definition of success matters, of course, if we do not survive as a race. We genuinely face the ultimate existential risk in the prospect of irreversible climate change causing the end of our species. The planet will find a way to recover, we may not. This threat will only be solved if we all work together, if we all include this aim in our ambitions and aspirations.

While we need to decarbonize, the exact solution is not yet totally known. What is clear is that this next decade is pivotal in both finding the solution and accelerating momentum towards Carbon Net Zero. For most of this book I will be encouraging you to generate your own definition of success, to think in a Maverick way. Here, though, there is some work that we *all* need to do, together, pulling in the same direction. This is prerequisite to allowing us to pursue the Maverick Path.

Mavericks were originally outside of society. The Modern Maverick is an evolution of this. A recognition that while we must define our own version of success, to be truly Maverick must include a positive contribution to those around us and to society as a whole. That is how we achieve meaning and ensure we survive.

The next decade is when we must build momentum, drive technological change, set examples for ourselves and our communities and lobby government. We need to do what we can at an individual level, at a business level and at a national and international level.

Our children will rightly turn around to us in years to come and ask what we did. This means whatever your individual measures of success are, they need to include having a positive impact on the world, whatever that means for you. This is our Second World War, our chance to be the next 'greatest generation'. This is hard, but we have to start somewhere. More detailed advice on where to start can be found on pages 150–3.

My Definition of Success

What might your first draft definition of success look like? Have a go at writing five aspects of what you would consider to be a successful life:

1. ....

2. ....

3. ....

4. ....

5. ....

Now you have a first pass at defining your version of success, go back through the list you made and drill down at least two levels. If you have written 'happy kids', for example, what do you mean by that? Keep asking yourself until you really have a clear answer. You might end up with something more detailed and useful, perhaps like this: a meaningful relationship with my children who are in the right school for them, forming friendships, developing their talents and understanding what good citizens look like.

In Summary

My summary of this chapter...

1. ....

2. ....

3. ....

Key Points

1. Without realizing it, we adopt unhealthy and unhelpful definitions of success.

2. We will not fulfil our potential and help others unless we have our own definition of success.

3. Any definition of success needs to include having a positive impact on our planet.

I am going to include here the summary of this chapter from an early reader of the book, as it is a helpful reflection: My takeaway is that unless you have ownership of what success looks like, it is impossible to live a conscious Maverick Life. By definition you are dependent on someone or something else and that removes your ability to be in control of your own success and happiness. Feeling like you are in control of your own success and happiness is enormously powerful – you become bulletproof to other people's judgement/behaviour.

CHAPTER SEVEN

Figuring Out Your Purpose

For most of us, living in a globally connected world where choices are infinite and capitalism is the dominant framework, it is incredibly difficult to figure out what really makes us tick. What is going to make us leap out of bed in the morning? (Well, *some* mornings anyway).

Purpose

What do you understand by the concept of purpose? Jot down a few lines of your thoughts here before we dive deeper:

....

....

....

....

....

Keep your definition in mind and let's look at some other definitions of purpose as it can mean many different things. The Chambers Dictionary states: 'Purpose is the reason for which something is done or created or exists'. Simon Sinek, author of the book *Start with Why:*

How Great Leaders Inspire Everyone to Take Action, says purpose is really the 'why', not the 'how' or 'what' we do.

Purpose creates the impact that we then derive our own sense of meaning from. Having a purpose to bring up children who contribute to society can be very meaningful. A job that helps manage pension funds to allow people to retire with security can also be meaningful, as can creating art that others enjoy. What is clear from all of this is that your purpose needs to be meaningful, i.e. bigger than yourself. Also, there needs to be self-regard or self-preservation in your purpose. Although the extreme example of giving up your life for another is meaningful, it does somewhat limit your ability to carry on living a life of, or on, purpose.

There are well-documented consequences of living a life not on purpose; the mid-life crisis being the most obvious example – 'I am not where I thought I would be', 'How did I end up doing this?', 'It's too late to change', 'I feel trapped' … all of these are comments I hear from clients and friends. Illness, burnout and even early death can be a consequence of living a purposeless life. A 2015 study in the *Lancet* by Professors Steptoe and Deaton showed that people with the greatest sense of purpose had a 30 per cent reduced risk of early death compared to those with the least sense of purpose.

Pause for a moment here. Having a clear purpose that is meaningful means:

- We are happier;
- We are helping others;
- We live longer.

So, we can see that living your purpose is like a turbo boost, unlocking another gear and taking you to another level. It is the only way to reach your full potential and to discover what is possible for you. If we all live our purpose, including our responsibility to the planet and our species, then we can and will survive as a race.

Living with your purpose helps navigate the ups and downs, to meet the challenges without buckling. Words like 'congruent' and 'authentic' are used increasingly in modern speech; you may think they've become meaningless buzzwords, but really what they both mean is, are you living a life true to your purpose? Purpose is another key underpinning of a Maverick Life.

Of course, work can be a major outlet for your purpose, but it's by no means the only one. If your purpose is to help others through honest conversations, then this does not switch off when you finish your working day. Sometimes, though, I see clients living a life of purpose *only* outside of work – the financier who does a lot of charity work, for example. I am never quite convinced by this.

Once tuned into your purpose you will be drawn to living it 24/7. It's not always possible, of course – the realities of life can get in the way and we know that some people have greater barriers than others to this kind of choice – but the less time you spend on purpose, the more likely it is that both your happiness levels and effectiveness will drop.

A useful way to think about purpose is that you will still be living it on your deathbed. For example, someone who has a purpose around reading, curating and making sense of world events will still be trying to read the papers and talk about what is going on in the world right to the end. They may well have had a career as a journalist, copywriter or academic. Likewise, someone who wants to care for others will still be trying to make sure that everyone (even those who are caring for them) is OK and as happy as possible. They could have been a doctor, nurse or carer. I will still be asking questions on my deathbed, interested in what is really going on for the people around me, how their lives are unfolding.

It is not always possible to live exactly on purpose. Imagine an archery target where your purpose is the bullseye; at times, you will be living close to your purpose, in the next ring out from the bullseye. This is OK. It's realistic and makes space for the other needs of life – like other people's purpose, or the need to eat, or to look after your health. What we want to avoid is living at the edge of the target, or even aiming your arrows at someone else's target. You cannot be fired from your purpose once you have discovered it.

When you are near your target, or even better, on target, a sense of effortlessness is felt. Things fall into place; openings arise and are taken. Often people say, 'Oh, they are so lucky, right place right time,' but what others might see as luck is often intention. Purpose provides a filter that shows you what to be open to, what to seek out and what to focus on. Work, on the whole, becomes enjoyable and time passes quickly. Thoughts of 'What am I going to do with my life?' recede and all that energy is channelled into productive forward motion. This effortlessness comes from a combination of using your strengths for activities that stir your soul and have meaning.

It is not straightforward to boil down your purpose. The question of why we are here has occupied philosophers for centuries. The modern world, from home to education to the workplace, is always showering us with ideas and messages of who we should be, what we should be doing and so on. Chopping down all these trees to reach the clearing that is really you is *hard*. To do so, we often need to go back to early childhood, when so much of our character and values are formed. We need to look at extreme moments in our lives, the peaks and troughs, and then analyse these and pick over them to find the themes.

This is probably the hardest exercise in the book and especially hard to do on your own. Involve a friend or a partner, do the exercise with them. Come back to this exercise as you work your way through the book. You are unlikely to nail it first or even second time around.

Purpose Finder

Think back over your life, especially to your childhood. Here are some starting questions for you to consider:

- What did you really love doing as a child? What did you always choose to do if left to your own devices?
- Think about two key moments in your life when you felt fulfilled – what were you doing and feeling? You can refer to your lifeline in Chapter 2 (*see also* page 17).
- If you had no constraints, no worries about money, family responsibilities or work that you felt bound to do, what would you love to spend the rest of your life working on?
- What problem faced by individuals or the world at large causes you the most concern?
- Which people in your life or beyond have inspired and taught you? What do you admire most in them?
- What do you really believe in?
- What is your superpower, something that you are genetically coded to do?

Now, here are some key questions for you to consider with input from others:

1. What do people come to you for? What skills do they ask for and what is it about your style that attracts them to you?
2. What comes naturally to you, so much so that you do it without thinking?
3. What would others who know you well say are your real contributions in life?
4. Who are the people in your life to whom you have contributed the most? How did you do so?
5. What are you doing when you seem at your happiest?

Ikigai+

As you complete these questions, you will start to see the idea of a life's work coming into play. To help further with this there is a Japanese model known as *Ikigai* (pronounced 'e-key-gai'). There is no direct translation into English, but the concept relates to 'a reason to live'. I have evolved the model to create the diagram below. I have used the Maverick expanded definition of work, not just what we can get paid for but what we can get rewarded for, financially or otherwise. I have also added the environment that you work in as a key factor to consider.

Think of four intersecting circles, which create a Venn diagram of different ways of using your time. There are activities or work which

1) you are passionate about
2) the world needs
3) you can be rewarded for
4) you are good at.

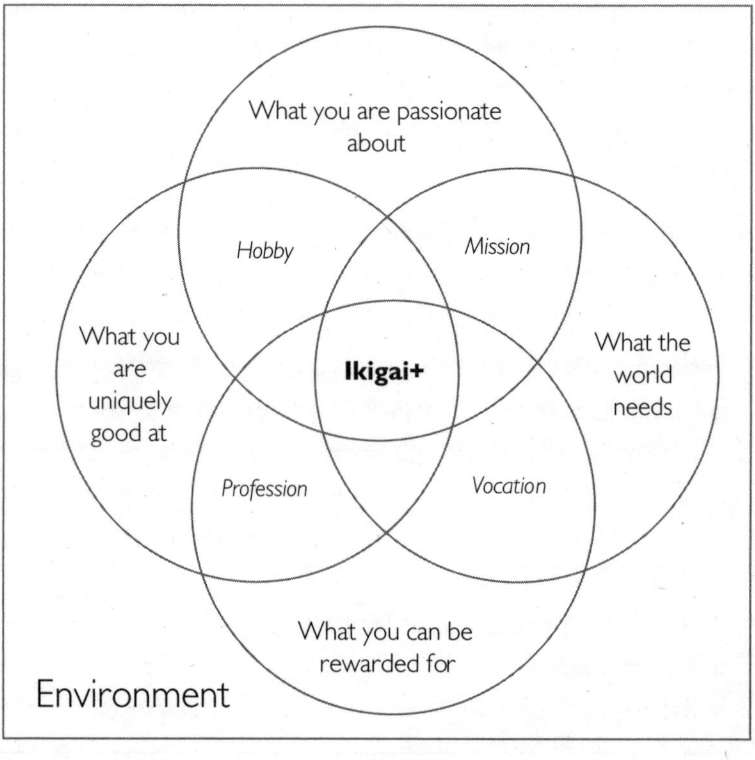

The area around the outside of the circles represents the environment you are doing the work in. Where is it? Who are you with? How do you travel there? All of these factors have an impact on finding and living a fulfilling life. You are thriving, living a Maverick Life, when you are living in the sweet spot of the four intersecting circles – this is Ikigai+, or purpose to use a Western word.

There are some pitfalls here, where two circles intersect. Consider the high-flyer: early on in their career, they find a great combination of work they are good at and that people pay well for. However, as the years progress, their trajectory seems to flatten out and others overtake them. They do not become leaders in their organizations, as they do not have the inbuilt passion for the work.

Jake was a consultant. A pretty good one but not a world-class one. Having figured out the system, he understood what was needed of him. He had friends at work and some of the work was interesting and challenging. He was earning a good salary, working hard and yet was utterly miserable. Jake had found a profession, one of several that he could be good at. The voice, his Inner Maverick, was getting louder, but he could not see a way out.

Jake had always been interested in people, in what made them tick. He noticed that the retail cases he consulted on were much more interesting (to him). Healthy and active, he was passionate about the outdoors. He was also risk averse and scared of setting out on his own. He had come close to opening a surf café, but it seemed just too big a leap from where he was, settled in a city with kids in local schools. Also, he was not sure that he could do it; did he have the right skills?

He figured out that he needed a bridge to the other side, but the chasm was too big and deep to just leap over so he took a job with a fast-growing retail business, not in an area he was passionate about, but as an apprenticeship. He loved it and learnt in six months more than he had learnt in five years as a consultant and at business school. He also made mistakes, but crucially with someone else's money and resources. He had tested and found a passion.

He was getting closer and the voice was still loud. He wanted more autonomy and to work in an area that he was passionate about, that the world needed. After joining forces with his wife, they went on to build an incredible company over the next 20 years that helped women become more active. They created the environment they both wanted to work in. Now he had Ikigai+, he had figured out his purpose. Not only that but he built a great marriage, he was also there for his kids and the hundreds of people who worked in the company. Everyone benefitted. Jake's Maverick move became a great multiplier of his talents and capabilities. For him the bridge was the key – his Maverick needed to run some experiments before taking the final leap.

Consider another overlap of two circles: those who use passion and strength to create amazing work that no one wants to pay for. Not only are they struggling financially, but in truth, their work is not even meaningful, as it is not having an impact on others. It is a purely selfish pursuit and ultimately not one that will make them happy. This can be known as a hobby. I explore later (*see also* page 95) the difference between a hobby and a purpose. If a hobby is something that the world needs and for which you can be rewarded, then that is a great purpose.

We also know people who are passionate about something which is not a strength. They pursue this for others at great expense to themselves, as it does not come naturally – this is a fast road to burnout.

So, what is your Ikigai+? Let's figure it out. Start with four blank circles, as in the diagram on page 72, with enough space to write different things in. You might even want to do this with a big sheet of paper and Post-it notes so you can move things around as you consider it.

Let's start with strengths. Strengths (what you are good at) can be intuited from your values or from times when you have been really flying: what were you doing in these moments? What comes naturally to you, what are you really, really good at? This is such a key question: what is unique to you, your absolute talent, something you were born to do? This is a key part of the Maverick Life – understanding your strengths and employing them in a purposeful way that benefits both you and others.

This takes some thinking about. Often clients will either say nothing or give a long list of rather generic answers, such as people, sales or being organized. Try to dig down to the next couple of levels and think about where you are uniquely talented. What aspect of building relationships are you particularly good at – is it quickly building trust or engaging people with humour? Go back to your purpose questions – what is it that people come to you for? If you have had 360-degree feedback or other psychometric tests from work, then study these too. Remember though that we are looking for strengths that are not just used at work; these may easily be talents you have outside of the office such as remembering lines, picking up new skills, processing large amounts of information and creating a story. Try to reduce the strength down to its key element.

If you would like a more scientific approach to this question, then you could take the VIA (Values in Action) strengths survey – it's easily found online and is a lovely way of describing strengths. When living our values, we are displaying our strengths. The top five VIA strengths are the ones that you will feel most at ease with when you are using them. My top strength is Honesty – useful in coaching when used carefully. Another in the top five is Love of Learning; I am happiest when I am reading or discussing new ideas.

The VIA strengths survey can also be useful in working on your own development goals – try looking at a strength in the 5–10 range on your ranking that you would like to work on. For this exercise, though, just focus on the top five to help you fill out your circles. Alternatively, use the Gallup Strengths finder under Services and Solutions at www.gallup.com (which is great, and very popular, but unlike VIA is not free).

Can you pick out one strength that is a superpower? Ask a few trusted people around you, what do you think my superpower is? You will receive some interesting answers. Often your superpower is what you do completely naturally without thinking. So, we do not spot these superpowers, we take them for granted. Clients have identified superpowers such as:

- communicating and staying calm under extreme pressure;
- making my children laugh;
- connecting people with the magic of the sea;
- being an external ambassador for the key messages of the business;
- extreme resilience;
- early-stage strategy for tech companies.

My superpower is quickly building a level of trust that allows me to ask direct questions. Once I had figured this out, I was able to head in the direction of coaching. You may be able to look backwards at activities that have had real meaning for you, where you have found a state of flow. Your strengths may be a mix of work and non-work, which is OK for now. Spend some time here, this is a key Maverick underpinning. Understanding our strengths and in particular our superpower gives us a huge advantage and sets us in the right direction. It is exhausting if the work you do or the life you lead does not engage your strengths – you will feel like a failure, that life is virtually impossible.

Ikigai+: Strengths

My strengths are ...

1. ....

2. ....

3. ....

4. ....

5. ....

My superpower is ...

....

....

Next, have a think about what you love doing, what you do for fun, what magazines you read, what you talk passionately about, what you would do if money was no object and what you will hopefully be doing until the day you die. Revisit the exercise you did on passions in Chapter 3 (*see also* page 28) – do you need to change anything?

Ikigai+: Passions

What I love doing is...

1. ....

2. ....

3. ....

4. ....

5. ....

Now, what do you do or could you do that the world needs? Start with a broad definition of need: parenting is clearly of value to your children, for example.

Which occupations have a positive impact on society as a whole? What skills are we short of? What are the biggest problems we face collectively?

Ikigai+: Needs

What I can do that the world needs…

1. ……………………………………………………

2. ……………………………………………………

3. ……………………………………………………

4. ……………………………………………………

5. ……………………………………………………

Finally, look for activities or jobs that you might be rewarded for. This could be financial if that is a priority or it might be recognition or love of some sort if, for example, you are caring for someone or teaching. At this stage, do not worry about how much you need to earn – we'll cover that later in the occupation pillar in Chapter 12. Think about your definition of success in Chapter 6 (*see also* page 64), how does this fit with what you will write below?

Ikigai+: Rewards

I can be rewarded for...

1 ....

2. ....

3. ....

4. ....

5. ....

Put your answers in the circles as in the diagram earlier (*see also* page 72), making sure to place things in the overlap sections where appropriate. What do you notice that sits in or near the middle of the diagram?

Finally, think about the environment you would like to work in. Inside or outside, at home or in an office, with others or on your own, near home or far away. Make a list of the factors that are important to you in your environment. We will use this list later in Chapter 12.

How is your purpose best expressed? I have found it useful to condense it into a phrase, something short and clear enough that it can be checked in with on a daily or weekly basis. As a simple template, you could capture in words:

- what it is that you offer;
- to whom;
- how it makes a difference.

For me, going through these questions, what became clear was that on my deathbed I would still be curious about how people were approaching their lives, how fulfilled they were, how Maverick were they? How happy they were and how I could help with that. What made them tick? Why did they behave in the way they behaved? I would still be asking questions. It is the thread that links back through all my life.

Thinking about language that is personal and meaningful to you is important here. I have heard some great catchphrases that others used, such as:

- 'Pick my line and launch' from a skier-turned-business leader, talking about how to make many decisions;
- 'You bring the fuel, and I provide the spark' from a coach who loved cars and engines;
- Jake, who was amazing at motivating and engaging others, used the phrase, 'Yes, we can'.

I spent many years of my life rowing and loved the river, the teamwork and the physical demands. Rowing is the only sport (other than synchronized swimming) where the team has to do the same thing at the same time. If you do it right, there is a magical moment when you are all perfectly in sync and the boat just takes off. I wanted to capture this in my purpose phrase and eventually came up with this catchphrase: 'Find our rhythm and fly'.

This phrase has sat well with me for several years now. I like the language (I always wanted to fly and soar and the key to fast rowing is rhythm). I like the fact it is a joint project (our rhythm) as I cannot achieve my purpose on my own; it's around helping others, so I need others to fulfil my purpose.

Now it's your turn to think about your purpose. Don't worry if it's hard; this will take time (mine took several weeks to emerge) but start here and revisit over the next few weeks. When it is right, the reaction from friends and family will be clear: 'Yes, that is definitely you'.

Purpose Statement

Finish this sentence:

My purpose is to…

....

....

If you need a prompt, try completing this phrase:

Because I believe in __________

I exist to ____________ (for people)

E.g. Because I believe in the power of human potential, I exist as a coach to help people find our rhythm and fly.

In Summary

My summary of this chapter…

1. ....

2. ....

3. ....

Key Points

1. Purpose provides a turbo boost that helps unlock your potential.
2. When you find it, you live your purpose all day, every day of your life.
3. This is a hard exercise that will take time and work to crack, but it is one of the five key underpinnings of a Maverick Life.

CHAPTER EIGHT

A First Look at the Life You Want

For this final chapter in Part II Dream, imagine having a magic wand that you can wave. Here, we are not interested in constraints or the realities of life but possibilities, in connecting with deep desires and longings that you have. In his book *The Five Longings: What We've Always Wanted – and Already Have*, David Richo talks about the longings that are in all of us:

- love
- meaning
- freedom
- happiness
- growth.

How does this list make you feel, what might be missing for you? What might you want more of?

One way of accessing some of your dreams is through visualization. What would you tell your younger self? This is one of the questions raised by the 80th Birthday Visualization Script (*see also* page 247). Through a series of prompts, it asks you to visualize your 80th birthday and then look back on the decades between then and 'now'. An extremely powerful exercise, clients are often in tears on completion and real insight is gained. It is almost always their favourite exercise when we work on Vision Days together. These are intense 1-2-1 days where through a variety of exercises a client confronts the three big questions facing them and looks to create a vision for their ideal future.

If you are already past your 80th birthday, then congratulations and feel free to imagine your 100th celebration.

80th Birthday

Have a go at the 80th-birthday exercise, either using the recording on the Modern Maverick website (www.themodernmaverick.com), or ask a friend or family member to facilitate by using the 80th Birthday Visualization Script in the Appendix (see also page 247). Afterwards debrief with yourself or your reader. You will need to write down or otherwise record the answers you come up with.

Where were you for your birthday? Was it somewhere you knew or somewhere you wanted to own? Who was there and who wasn't there? Who made a speech, if anyone did at all? What was happening during the different decades of your life, what did you notice changing?

What emerged for you? What was your piece of wisdom? And perhaps more pertinently: what makes it so hard to listen to this wisdom now? We will study this more in Chapter 14, but for now, just treasure the advice from your 80-year-old self. It is worth writing down and always having near you.

In my experience, the most powerful question is: 'What would your 80-year-old self say to your self today?' The answers cluster around three themes:

1) You are going to be OK, everything is going to be OK
2) Lighten up, stop taking things so seriously
3) Spend time on the important things.

What do these themes say to you, do they resonate? Are they similar to your own piece of wisdom? It is amazing what our subconscious will tell us if we ask it in a sufficiently relaxed and open state.

Be honest with yourself – what was revealed, perhaps about the place you are living or want to live. The work you are doing or the people you are spending your time with. Confront this. It does not mean you have to make sweeping changes immediately, more that this feeds into your overall Maverick Plan, which will be shaped through the book.

A second way of starting to think about the life you want is to write a stop, start and continue doing list. Three columns where you can write down the activities or people or places that you would like to stop, start, or continue doing. The list is not based on the realities of life today but what your life could be like without constraints. We can tackle the constraints later, for now keep dreaming.

A final way of building your dream vision is to start to imagine your perfect week. We will look at this in more detail in Chapter 16 but for now, make a list of what would be in your perfect week or even perfect month. What surprises you? What would you like to do more of? What would you like to do less of?

We're coming to the end of the Dream section and now is the time to start pulling together the amazing work you have done in the first two parts of this book. Before moving on to Part III Do, I recommend that you start reading back through the exercises you have completed. It is worth taking a separate piece of paper, or your special notebook if you are a stationery addict.

Jot down comments or answers that surprise you as you read through. Also note ideas of through-lines that might start to show or illustrate a potential sense of direction. Are there any clear themes starting to emerge? It is OK to be free form at this stage, the final detailed plan will emerge later in the book.

Revisit your three-sentence living eulogy from the introduction (*see also* page xv) and perhaps expand it by a few sentences. What has changed for you since the beginning of the book? What do you notice as you start to read?

A final question to mull on: What would you do if you knew you simply could not fail?

....

....

....

....

In Summary

My summary of this chapter…

1. ....

2. ....

3. ....

Key Points from Parts I and II, Discover and Dream

Here are the key points from the first two parts of the book – take a moment to review before moving on.

1. The Modern Maverick looks for a more autonomous way of living, creating the life they love and believe in.
2. In doing so, they benefit not just themselves but those around them and society at large, changing the world around them.
3. The exercises are a key part of the Maverick Path – find a way to do as many of them as you can.
4. Growth and change are not possible without self-enquiry.
5. We need others' input to increase our self-awareness.
6. We can hold ourselves back with our beliefs and stories; we let false truths dominate our thinking. These can be modified.
7. A small number of key moments have a large impact on your life.
8. Positive or negative, it is how we deal with the moment, rather than the moment itself, that determines our future happiness.
9. Left unexamined and unprocessed, negative life events will have a deleterious future effect.
10. Your values are fixed early in life and are your operating system – they really matter.
11. These values determine what and who you will enjoy spending time on.
12. Once you understand this you can intentionally design how you spend your time.
13. It is useful to assess where you are currently on a set of key life pillars.

14. For a happy, healthy life, there needs to be a balance and good scores across the three areas and 12 pillars – this is Life Fit.
15. A low overall score indicates the need for major change or revolution, while individual low scores show areas for evolution.
16. Most of us spend too much time worrying about what others think and comparing ourselves to false impressions of others.
17. The Maverick looks for internal measures of success rather than relying on external validation.
18. Other people have more than enough of their own stuff to worry about.
19. Without realizing it, we adopt unhealthy and unhelpful definitions of success.
20. We will not fulfil our potential and help others unless we have our own definition of success.
21. Any definition of success needs to include having a positive impact on the planet.
22. Purpose provides a turbo boost that helps unlock your potential.
23. When you find it, you live your purpose all day, every day of your life.
24. This is a hard exercise that will take time and work to crack, but it is one of the five key underpinnings of a Maverick Life.
25. We tend to take things too seriously, with unnecessary levels of anxiety.
26. We can lose touch with our dreams, with those early aspirations that are often deeply connected to who we are.
27. Our wise 80-year-old self is present in our current selves and can act as an excellent guide.

PART III

Do

CHAPTER NINE

The Maverick Path

We now move on to a more practical section of the book. You have already done a great deal of self-analysis and tackled some extremely hard questions around purpose, definition of success and strengths. The first two parts of this book covered the initial three steps towards a Maverick Life:

1) Defining your own version of success
2) Identifying your strengths and in particular your superpower
3) Deciding how and where to apply those strengths – your purpose.

The next two sections cover the last two steps:

4) Using the Life Quotient (LQ) tool to become Life Fit and highly effective
5) Creating, testing and refining your Maverick Plan to guarantee progress with your Maverick Life.

Principles of Happiness

One of the most overused and least understood phrases in the English language is 'work-life balance'. There is so much conflicting thought and advice. Blur the work/life boundary, don't blur it, make your hobby your work and so on. What is work and what is life and what is balance? Where does parenting or volunteering fit in? One sure fact is that most of us feel we do not have a good work/life balance. A survey I ran in

2015 showed people on average reporting their work/life ratio as 75/25 with a desired ratio of 55/45. That is a big shift, the equivalent of more than a day per week moving from work to life.

Let's assume most of us have 100 awake and alert hours per week. This is roughly a 14-hour day, allowing for the all-important eight hours for sleep and an hour either side of that to wake up and to wind down, wash and take on board some food. Now grab a piece of paper and allocate your 100 hours based on an average of the last month between three areas:

- Work – your primary occupation, paid or unpaid
- Self – time dedicated to you, selfish time if you like
- Others – time dedicated to others, friends, family; for now, let's include parenting and caring in here.

Now draw a circle and divide it up into three areas in proportion to what you have allocated above. If you are in the main throes of your career it may look like the left-hand circle; if you are a part-time parent, it may resemble the right-hand one. This is the Pie of Life:

Career focus

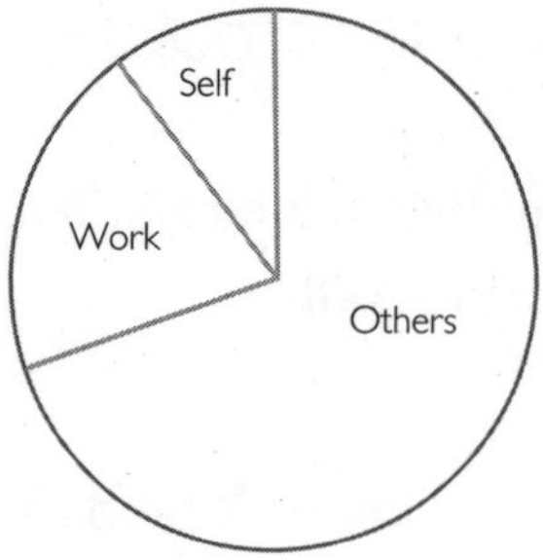

Parenting/caring focus

What do you notice? Of course, in each case, it is self that is squeezed. This is the one that shouts quietest, the one that can be taken from without letting others down, the one easiest to say 'no' to. We all experience this: feeling tired, not taking as much exercise as we want to, meditation and yoga being a dream rather than a reality, time to read our book or practise the piano or take a walk never quite materializing. Sometimes we will even reduce sleep to try and allocate more time to others or work.

If the charts above show an imbalance, what does a 'good' balance look like? Well, the experts suggest that to have a harmonious life (we are going to quietly drop the word 'balanced' here as it torments most of us), each of the three slices of the pie needs to be roughly equal, as shown below. That's 33⅓ hours on each slice per week. Thirty-three hours on work and 33 hours on self. It may sound completely crazy but stay with me. At the time of writing, France has a mandated working week of 35 hours and on average in the UK, people work 36.4 hours per week, with 48 hours as the maximum mandated. The problem with averages of course is that it smooths out both extremes, 16 per cent of people in the UK work over 45 hours per week leaving little or no time for themselves or others.

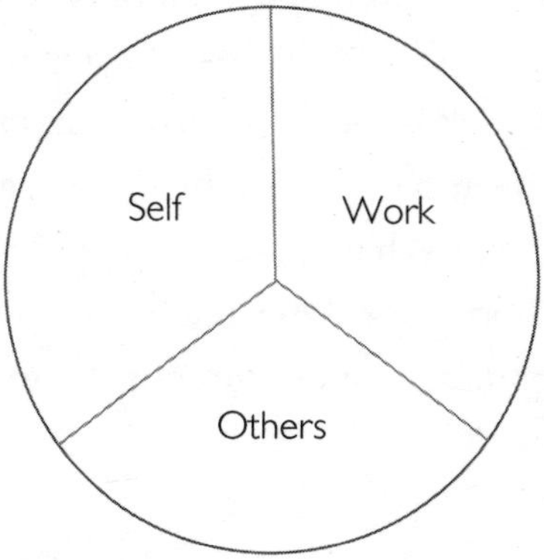

Harmonious life

So how to go about this? First, remember this is an ideal not a command, so be kind to yourself. Let's also remember that if you're aged around 30 to 55, you are probably in the busiest period of your life, where work, career and earning are competing for your time with parenting, partnering and ageing parents, let alone your friends or your own needs. Let's not put more pressure on.

We can return to our definitions: what is Work, Others and Self? How about this? If we are a primary carer for children or others, then defining this as our main occupation means we can move this time into Work, instead of Others. This is likely to even things up immediately. Now, let's look at the crucial aspect of any 'Work', which is building and maintaining our network of relationships. Let's move this into Others and take it out of Work. So now the balance between these two may be a little more even – great. But my guess is that Self is still extremely squeezed. So how do we start to build up slowly and deliberately towards 33 hours of Self per week, or a number more realistic for ourselves?

First of all, let's look at why Self is so important. We are often programmed against being selfish but if we do not look out for ourselves, we have nothing left to give to others – the irritable parent, the half-asleep manager is not helpful. The irony is that by spending more time on Self, not only do we have a more enjoyable life, but we are also able to give more in the other areas, to achieve more in less time. So, knowing now that Self is the most important of the three life areas, that it enables us to be at our best in the other areas, how then do we grow this slice of the pie? What makes us happy?

What do happy people do? After reading far too many studies on how to achieve happiness, some common themes of happy people seem to emerge. They…

- devote a great amount of time to their family and friends, nurturing and enjoying those relationships
- are comfortable expressing gratitude for all they have
- are often the first to offer a helping hand to co-workers and passers-by
- practise optimism when imagining their futures
- spend time outdoors

- savour life's pleasures and try to live in the present moment
- make physical exercise a weekly and sometimes daily habit
- are deeply committed to lifelong goals and ambitions (e.g. fighting fraud, building cabinets or teaching their children their own deeply-held values)
- sleep more
- develop a meditation practice
- help others – 100 hours per year seems to have the maximum impact
- have their share of stresses, crises and even tragedies. They may become just as distressed and emotional in such circumstances as you or I, but their secret weapon is the poise and strength they show in coping in the face of challenge.

What strikes you on reading this list? What is missing? Overthinking, ruminating and navel gazing do not appear. There is much evidence to suggest that rumination not only prevents happiness but can lead to depression. Psychologists Lyubomirksy and Lepper found that depression worsens if rumination is created as part of the experiment. Sitting alone and declaring, 'I want to be happier and I'm going to figure out how' simply makes things worse. Staring happiness in the eye, much like Medusa, may turn you to stone. Instead, as with the list above, pursuing a group of positive intentional activities for the right reasons will lead to an increase in happiness as a by-product, *not* an end product.

In Chapter 3, I mentioned having a hobby as 'work' (*see also* page 28) – does it help you live a more holistic and happy life if you work on your hobby, or make your hobby your main source of income? From my work with clients, I've observed that this does not seem to be as satisfying as anticipated. The definition of a hobby is something done for pleasure; when you put pressure on yourself to earn money from doing your hobby or to make the hobby meaningful, the enjoyment seems to fade away. Think of the literary agent who never reads for pleasure or the pianist who never plays at home anymore. The hobby is there as an escape, something that is meaningful to you not necessarily to others and belongs firmly in the Self bucket. It does not need to serve a higher purpose or bring in cash, it is there to help you achieve balance and fulfilment.

Autonomy

There are two further key aspects to living a Maverick Life, autonomy and risk taking. Autonomy is the ability to decide how to live your life. Psychologists Ryan and Deci define autonomy as volition, 'having the experience of choice and endorsing one's actions at the highest level of reflection'. Remember the internal vs external motivations in Chapter 5 (*see also* page 49)? Autonomy is about making internally motivated decisions. The idea is both to be intentional in what you do and to be able to flex and change when inevitably that plan does not work out as expected. It gives us the ability to choose where we spend our time and energy, the key underpinning of the Maverick Life.

Research in 2022 by Kukita and colleagues published in the *Journal of Positive Psychology* shows that experiencing autonomy is a key contributor to a good life. Their research found that the level of autonomy their participants experienced had a significant impact on happiness and well-being. Importantly, this impact was across all three aspects that psychologists use to define happiness:

- Affect (emotion and mood)
- Engagement
- Meaning.

Kukita and co. contrasted autonomy with the impact of activity types (work, study, play, rest) and found it was the only significant predictor for affect and engagement and the strongest predictor for meaning.

Choosing to do something is more important than the actual activity in determining your happiness and well-being. OK, re-read that last sentence and pause for a moment. Having choice is more important than what you choose. This is about you being the pilot of your life, not the passenger. At some level, we all have a choice: we can carve out autonomy. Even within our existing lives there are ways of increasing our level of conscious thought and deliberate action.

Take a look back at the lifeline that you drew in Chapter 2 (see also page 17). Label up the points where you had the most autonomy and where you were most in charge of your life. What do you notice? What are the patterns? What preceded a good period on the lifeline? While it's not impossible to live a life of autonomy as part of a large organization, it does require a level of seniority and/or a culture that celebrates output instead of input; one that allows you to do the work as and when it is most effective for you. It also requires a culture that supplies the necessary resources to support staff and does not trap its team in a perpetual cycle of overwhelm.

So, is the obvious route to be your own boss, then? Well, possibly, but it's not always that simple: there is a different but equally dangerous trap lying in wait here. Instead of your business working for you, you can end up working endlessly for your business. I'm sure we all know that entrepreneur or freelancer who is constantly on, a slave to their email and their team (or a lack of one) so it's not a totally clear-cut distinction. Fundamentally, though, autonomy is easier when you are your own boss.

A study in 2017 by Peter Warr at the University of Sheffield and Ilke Inceoglu at the University of Exeter found that self-employed people are happier and more engaged in their work than those in any other profession. People who are self-employed say that it's the freedom, flexibility, control and sense of purpose that makes them happier. Looking at it like this, perhaps it's not such a surprise; I believe we are all born with these innate desires. When you watch a two-year-old being told that they cannot do something, the strong reaction is due to these core desires being curtailed. Ultimately, this is about us being ourselves; being *true* to ourselves.

In 2016, PwC conducted a wide-ranging study called 'Work 3.0 – understanding how we'll work next'. They found 43 per cent of people working in small companies (<50 employees) felt happy at work vs 27 per cent of those in large organizations (>1,000 employees). To be honest, it's not the difference that strikes me most, it's that *both* numbers seem too low to me, given how much time we spend working. The gap between happiness at small and large companies was attributed to less bureaucracy, tighter cultures and leniency around work policies like flexible hours and working from home in smaller companies – in other words, there was more autonomy in the smaller companies.

The key number, though, is that 86 per cent of respondents at least somewhat agree that they have a strong desire to work independently – an overwhelming majority. This is driven by a perception that independent work gives greater flexibility, control over your working environment, the opportunity to earn more and have a more harmonious life. The main detractor from this is the 39 per cent who say that uncertainty of income is the least appealing aspect of freelancing; while you may gain autonomy, you lose your safety net. Despite this barrier, people have acted: there are 150 million independent workers across the US and Western Europe. Very few of them talk about yearning to go back to an organization.

What is clear is that as workers, we *want* to be more self-directing and trends such as longevity and the growth in the gig economy mean that we will *have* to be more self-directing. This does not have to be just for the self-employed, although this is of course the ultimate expression of self-direction. Within the workplace you can increasingly job-craft. The idea was coined by Amy Wrzesniewski and colleagues at Michigan Ross School of Business. It involves redefining your job to incorporate your motives, strengths and passions – essentially, taking an entrepreneurial attitude to employed work, to try and get the best of both worlds. You can be a Maverick job-crafter, rather than settle for a bullshit job.

So, do you have what it takes to make the leap to independent work? Many of us also follow independent work because we have to. We must relocate for some reason, or care for someone, or cannot find work that fits with when or what we want to do.

Those Mavericks that choose independent work tend to be driven by a desire to innovate, to make things better and disrupt the status quo. You need an ability to sell, whether products to customers, ideas to your team or a vision that you have created to potential hires and investors. A level of self-belief that allows a thirst for learning and feedback, the ability to bounce back from the inevitable failures and a flexibility that is crucial in the early stages of establishing a business. A resourcefulness and an ability to be proactive, nothing happens unless you make it happen. Some level of emotional intelligence and ability to work with others. A high level of grit and persistence. Finally, and perhaps the most important, is an understanding of your risk appetite.

Risk Taking

Given risk is probably the largest barrier to starting out on your own, how can you safely explore the idea? This is something I come across in client work a lot – it is often a client's perceived sense of risk that stops them from acting. When we dig into the actual risk – the difference between reality and perception – the constraints tend to fall away.

Consider Amy, a successful lawyer at a fast-growing firm. She has young kids and yearns for more freedom. Her perceived risk is that on leaving the security of her employment, she will enter a vacuum, not have the skills to earn money or even know what to do. We work on really testing those limiting beliefs; what are the *real* risks and how can she mitigate those risks? Suddenly, she has a transition plan, with a clear leaving date, ideas about how she could develop opportunities during that transition period and how she makes the most of her current role to help with the transition.

Overblown perceived risks are a sure way of keeping us in our current role, a safety blanket that means we avoid taking any actual risks. It is human nature to overestimate risk, as this is what kept our ancestors safe and alive. But we don't have to be dictated to by our instincts: sit with a friend and ask them to really challenge you on what the actual risks are of your idea. How could you find out more about the risks? What could you do to mitigate them?

Moving to working on your own is probably the lowest-risk way of increasing your freedom. As you move from being self-employed to creating a business or organization that is larger than you, then risk does increase, because identifying opportunities and trying to capture value from these opportunities involves taking on capital (external or internal), expanding products and geographies, and increasing your reliance on others. You need a balanced sense of risk and a proactive approach to managing risks that you can identify and control.

Being an entrepreneur is not right for everyone – we will use a diagnostic tool in Chapter 12 (page 163) to help you figure this out. If you do decide to stay in your current role, or that paid work is not central to your life right now, that is fine. Being a maverick is about living *your* best life and making free choices – not becoming a cookie-cutter version of an entrepreneur if that does not suit you.

Why is it so important that you make changes now? Three key reasons. First, if you have read this far, then you clearly have a great desire to shift the focus of your life but have not yet been able to do so. It is time to act, that gnawing feeling you have is only going to grow stronger. You may have been waiting for the right call, the right voice… well, if you are still reading, then you have found it.

The second reason is those around you. If you have been focused on the wrong metrics, chasing a false version of success, you will have damaged or limited the relationships closest to you. Those people, particularly if they are your actual dependants, need you. They deserve the best of your energy and spirit, not what is left over after a draining day of emails and meetings.

There is a third and even more important reason why the world needs Mavericks, now more than ever. Today, we face a universal existential threat like never before. We have only one planet. We cannot afford to continue sleepwalking through jobs that do not liberate our strengths and creativity, that have no meaning or purpose beyond getting paid. The chart below gives some samples of re-evaluating what we take to be important:

Non-Maverick	**Maverick**
Likes and followers	Close friendships
Income and bank balance	Enough (money)
Titles and profile	Inner validation
Busyness	Inner peace
Personal bests	Sustainable health
Hacking	Mastery
Networks	Community
Objects	Experiences
Self-promotion	Outward vulnerability
Bingeing	Moderation
Drugs and alcohol	Meditation and therapy
Work	Family
Job	Life's work
Passenger	Pilot

They have a word in Danish, *nok*, that means 'enough'. Although their society is changing, there are still few displays of wealth: cars in Copenhagen are modest, and there is no international art scene as people do not see the point in paying huge sums for art that others recognize. They have a concept of taking only enough for what their family needs, within reason. 'Enough' is a strong Maverick concept.

Time to get started. One of the benefits of my short stint as an elite athlete was an understanding of what was possible and what could happen through the compounding impact of smaller, regular training sessions. There is an extraordinary payoff that comes from focused dedication; changes that are not seen on a daily basis, but become clear over weeks, months and years.

The following three chapters provide ideas and guides to what those training sessions might look like across 12 key pillars of being Life Fit. As you work through them you can either read all the way through or prioritize areas that scored low on your LQ metric in Chapter 4 (*see also* pages 35–40). I would, though, recommend reading about some good scores as well as lower scores – to make sure you get a clear picture and a rounded idea of your path.

My summary of this chapter...

1. ....

2. ....

3. ....

Key Points

1. Work dominates our lives without us realizing it – we need to reprioritize self and others we care about.
2. Mavericks need to create autonomy to have intentional lives. Even if we do not start our own businesses, we can live in a more entrepreneurial way.
3. We can stop at enough, it is the external motivations that keep us striving unnecessarily.

CHAPTER TEN

Self

A current trend is towards hyper-individualism; too much 'me' and not enough 'we'. It's strange then, perhaps, to begin this next section of the book with a look at 'self', which contains the first four pillars. Without the self, though, there is no ability to help others or leave the world in a better place. Too much self and the profits of life are at risk of being kept for personal gain; too little self and there are no profits at all – there is only exhaustion, burnout and ultimately an early demise. Although we rail against the selfish elite, the foolish saint is almost as much of a problem. This is the person who gives, gives and gives, without focusing on those who they can most help, and without protecting themselves. Yes, their candles burn brightly, but not for long enough.

Self consists of mind and body. You cannot be strong in one without the other. They are completely linked through our nervous systems. A stressed mind can impact the body through the immune system, digestion, skin conditions, pain and fatigue. The Maverick works on both mind and body.

It is a shame that the phrase 'self-care' has become so overused and mocked, because there can be no Maverick without self-care. Carving one's own path takes energy, flexibility and agility. This is not idling or languishing in the comfort zone of life. To be at the best of your ability means being Life Fit and understanding what it takes to do that. Where do you think you are now? How charged are your batteries? Use the chart on the next page to plot where you are now and where you would like to be…

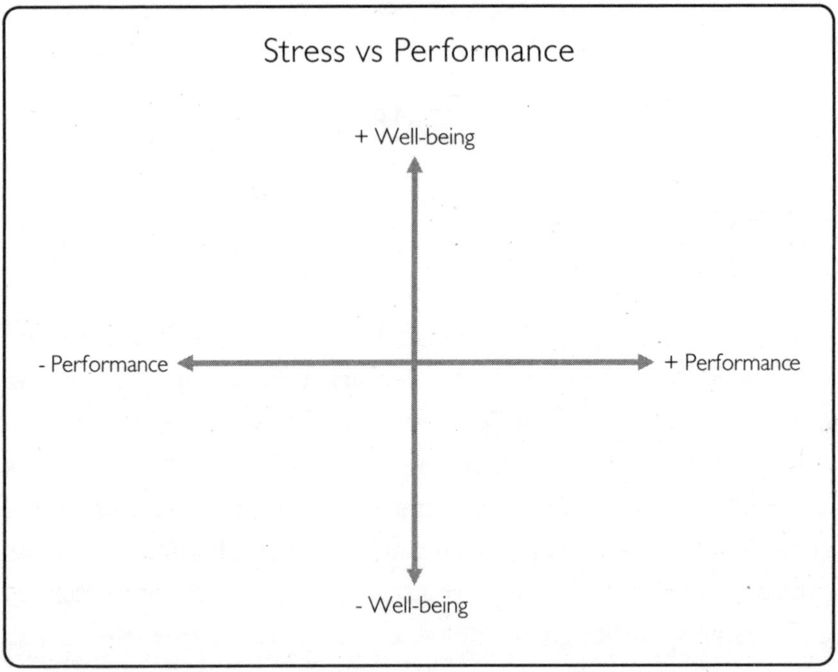

We often chase performance at the expense of our well-being. Ignoring our well-being means that over time our performance drops and we end up in the lower left area of the chart.

Many of us hover around long-term fatigue, occasionally tipping into illness, and even less frequently finding a period of rest and calm. The long-term play is around creating a set of habits and controlling the overall pace, so that the normal state is in the sweet spot between idleness and burnout, our best possible selves. This is when we sit up in the top right hand corner of the chart above.

This is a concept from the field of Positive Psychology, where you imagine your best possible self in a potential future where almost everything has gone well. Multiple studies have found this exercise beneficial, such as Heekerens and Eid at the University of Berlin (2020).

Take a few minutes to imagine things going right. Where are you, who are you with, what is happening around you? What is work, what is life? Now write this down as a few bullet points.

Best Possible Self

My best possible self is...

....

....

....

....

....

This is a chance to let go of the tough expectations that we set ourselves and subsequently fail on. We really are our own worst enemies. As you read through the next four pillars, rather than judging yourself or looking at where you come up short, celebrate the areas you do well in and start a list of the areas you would like to work on. There's no rush: this is your life's work, after all.

Pillar 1: State of Mind – Our Beliefs and Attitude

As we start to look at each pillar in turn it is a good idea to go back to your LQ answers (*see also* Chapter 4, pages 35–40). Check in with the score and your responses for each pillar before reading the relevant section as it will prime your mind to start thinking about changes you can make.

We all run stories in our heads. Stories about who we are, where we come from, what others think of us, why we do what we do. These stories, often referred to as 'schema' in psychology, are beliefs that we hold about ourselves and it turns out they are incredibly powerful.

Formed most often during our childhoods, we tend to look for data that reinforces these stories throughout our lives. This is one of the reasons why two people seeing the same thing can experience it in completely different ways. We looked at your stories in Chapter 1 (*see also* page 5).

Here's a quick example to illustrate. Imagine you are giving a lecture; you are a bit nervous as it's the first time you have talked to such a large audience. Five minutes in, the person in the front row barely manages to stifle an enormous yawn. What is your reaction?

a) I must be boring
b) They must have been up all night, partying
c) Stutter to a halt and leave the stage
d) Poor them, maybe they have been up all night with a newborn and are trying to study at the same time to further their prospects.

Those of us (little Ed included) who carry around the story 'I am not good enough' immediately assume the answer is (a). Depending on how strongly this has been imprinted during childhood, and how we have tackled this since, we may even follow through with (c). However, those whose story is 'I can do this' or 'I am good at what I do' will tend to jump to (b) or (d). The difference is a belief about causation: rather than jumping to the belief that I caused the yawn, there may be a series of outside factors beyond my control that caused it.

Our early experiences and our stories can push us towards a passive acceptance of life, or a proactive attempt to create the life we want. Consider for a moment the nuance between 'life is tough' and 'life is challenging' (we do not often hear people say, 'life is easy'). 'Life is tough' implies an abdication of agency; an experience of being done to. This is what psychologist Martin Seligman described as 'learned helplessness'. Whatever I do it does not work, so why bother? Life is just unfair. The elite just get richer and there is nothing I can do about it. That makes me angry and bitter, so I give up.

'Life is challenging' is a more realistic assessment. Challenges can be overcome, can be worked with. Pleasure and happiness are derived from tackling challenges, often more than from times of plain sailing. Fundamentally, we have a choice: be a victim of our past or an architect of our future. Architects make changes, they make things happen. Entrepreneurs are architects – although a person may have worked to reach this attitude, rather than being naturally born with it. They have somehow turned this around into a sense of 'can do' rather than 'done to'. This shift happens when negative stories are modified and positive stories amplified.

So how do we work with our stories? Can we change them? The news from Seligman is positive. Instead of learned helplessness, we can learn and practise optimism. Not only does this lead to a reduction in depression and more joy in life, it also helps us run through the metaphorical brick walls in our way and make things happen.

Here are two different ideas to experiment with. First, how do we know when a negative story is running? We become emotionally activated. In extreme circumstances, we will sweat, have a higher heart rate or even faint. More likely we just feel a little agitated or threatened, and there is that feeling in the pit of our stomach as our adrenaline is released. Next time you feel like this, try and identify the story that is running. Take the lecture as an example. The story that kicks in for me is 'I am boring and no one is interested in what I say, it has always been so, who am I to even be on this stage?' Now try running a different story: 'There are 99 other people here who are not yawning, I know that there are times when people have been interested in what I say, I am just going to go for it'.

What impact do the two different stories have on the rest of the lecture? Significant. If I allow the first story to run, I will be more nervous and less convincing and interesting. Nervousness is not a helpful communication tool. The story makes things worse (this is why they become so powerful and entrenched, they are self-reinforcing). The second story grows my confidence and helps me deliver a better lecture, and chips away at the old story.

But it's not about being falsely positive; for example, let's say lots of people were yawning or walking out of the lecture. The answer is not to blindly convince yourself that you are still great and interesting, but to make an honest appraisal. Did I under prepare? Do I know enough about the topic, did I get the audience wrong, am I better in smaller, more intimate discussions rather than lectures? This does not imply you are a total failure, more that there is not a fit between your superpower and what the audience needs.

Shifting stories is not easy; these are deeply-held, entrenched beliefs. However, it is *possible* and taking responsibility for your stories is the starting point. If you are struggling to spot or change your stories then a therapist can be incredibly helpful, in particular a relatively new form of psychotherapy called Schema Therapy. This is an integrated approach combining several different disciplines to help you ensure your emotional needs are met in a helpful way.

Stress

Stress is a silent killer. I think that one day we will look back on stress like many of us now look on tobacco – why would you start smoking today, knowing the impact on your health and wallet? But for now, we live in a VUCA world: volatile, uncertain, complex and ambiguous. With current political and social events, this is only increasing, and what's more, we are constantly connected through technology to this world. We are expected (mainly by ourselves) to deliver at an exceptional standard and of course we must respond instantly. No wonder we're stressed.

Stress is caused both by external factors (situations or threats or changes that required adaptation) and by internal factors (our own dialogue, our personal resilience). We can also 'catch' stress from others. Have you wondered why you yawn when someone else does? These are our mirror neurones at work; the parts of our brains which mimic others, to help us fit in and form connections. Although crucial in development and relationships, they can also be a conduit for absorbing other people's stress. Perhaps reduce the interactions with the stress conductors in your life, if you can.

Stress arises when our perception of what is needed of us is greater than our perception of the resources available to us. There are some clues in this sentence to reduce stress. First, we need to check our perceptions. Are they real? Do we really have to do what we think we have to do? Do we only have the resources we think we have? Then we have two options to reduce stress; reduce what is needed of us by saying no, delegating or other methods, or increase the resources at our disposal by asking for help or buying relevant equipment or software, for example.

As a slight aside, I am sometimes asked the difference between worry and anxiety. Simply put, worry is *productive* stress: it occupies you for up to an hour a day and triggers problem solving and action. It is temporary and centres around realistic concerns. Anxiety is ongoing, occupies five hours per day or more and leads to feelings of hopelessness and paralysis. It is often felt in the body rather than the head. This is unproductive stress. If you feel this way, it is best to consult your GP – this book is not a substitute for proper medical intervention for a potential mental illness.

So, what to do about this problem of stress? First, let's take a step back. Stress is not always bad; some stress has an evolutionary function, to help us perform. The ideal level of stress seen on the chart below is when we are in our comfort and stretch zones. This helps us perform at our best.

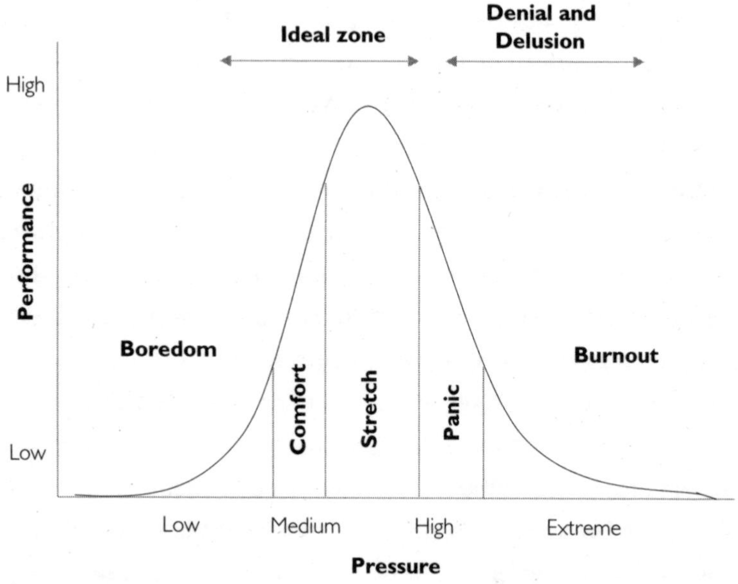

However, extreme or prolonged stress can be very detrimental. Not only does our performance drop, but our health is also quickly impacted. It's like running your car with the accelerator permanently floored; eventually the engine will blow. Have a quick think about how stressed you are right now. Where would you place yourself on a scale of 1–10, with 10 being very stressed? What would your average score be over the last year? If you want to take a more detailed stress test, I recommend checking out the ISMA survey, which can be found online and is produced by the International Stress Management Association (under free downloads in the What is Stress section at www.isma.org.uk).

There are several self-inflicted reasons that make us more prone to stress:

- Control – trying to do everything ourselves and trying to control the un-controllables, or on the other hand, a completely out-of-control feeling
- Perfectionism – being highly self-critical, with impossibly high standards

- Responsibility – assuming we can change everything
- Low self-protection or low resilience
- Identity and rest of life very dependent on a narrow definition of success (e.g. work)
- Negative self-talk ('I know this is going to go badly', 'I'm so stupid, I'll never succeed').

The ancient Greek philosophers known as the Stoics thought a lot about this. They were a very practical school of philosophy and are having a renaissance today as they provide extremely clear guidance to reduce stress. The key principle is to be clear on what is under our control and to focus on this. Much of our stress, they argue, is caused by focusing on external factors beyond our control.

There are also evolutionary reasons why we feel stressed. The amygdala is one of the older parts of our brain and controls our fight-or-flight response. This is often called the 'amygdala hijack' – it overrides our newer, more rational parts of the brain. Combined with the vagal nerve it forms part of our sympathetic nervous system, which minimizes brain function and operates the subconscious fight, flight or freeze responses. Only nowadays, there is no lion to run away from, so the same response is triggered by our email inbox. Adrenaline is the hormone that triggers fight or flight, but when this goes on for a longer time frame, cortisol is released. Both hormones have a purpose and are useful in the functioning of our brains and bodies. When cortisol levels remain high for prolonged periods, this creates problems.

The other part of the autonomic nervous system is the parasympathetic. When we are in states governed by this system we rest, digest, feed and breed. It also controls self-repair. Vital for maintaining health, both mental and physical, it cannot operate at the same time as the sympathetic system. The effects of extreme stress – too much from your sympathetic nervous system – are felt in all areas of life. We will be more forgetful and make worse decisions.

We will feel anxious and tearful and change the way we eat. We may have panic attacks, aches and pains, bowel problems, palpitations and become ill frequently. We can withdraw from others, become aggressive and lose our sense of humour. And, of course, we sleep badly. If you feel any of these symptoms for more than five days in a row, you need to make a change.

But – I hear you say – it is not that bad, I am just going to keep going. I'm coping just fine. Well, maybe… but probably not. Around 70 per cent of visits to the doctor and 85 per cent of serious illnesses are linked to stress. Anxiety increases the chance of depression and heart attacks and is increasingly linked to the growth of cancerous cells. Nobel Prize winner Elizabeth Blackburn and psychologist Elisabeth Epel have found that constant stress wears down our telomeres, the caps of our DNA that protect our cells from illness and ageing. To top it all, stress shrinks your brain. Keep it up for long enough and your body will step in and take the choice out of your hands: this is when people experience a breakdown. Working with people in this situation, it takes them a minimum of three to six months to return to work and normally a different type of work. It's a serious thing and a major derailing of a move to a Maverick Life – don't let yourself end up there.

Lee was a client who worked in TV and came to me with high stress levels and problems with sleeping. His confidence was low and his performance and decision-making were suffering. He was very focused on future events that might happen and spent most of his time thinking up and focusing on worst-case scenarios. He was trapped and feeling stuck. We talked about times when he did feel in control and was performing at his best. He described an almost-different person when he was in Los Angeles – he was much more confident and had a can-do approach. We called this person 'LA Lee' and had him look at Lee's current life. LA Lee could see where Lee was worrying unnecessarily and stopping himself from moving forward. He realized that he was externalizing everything and making himself into a helpless victim. By focusing on what he could control, he began to move forward and build momentum.

What can we do? Often, we cannot remove the external factors (our jobs, commuting, family) but we can change the way we choose to react to these stressors. We can accept that we cannot control everything and that sometimes good enough is better than perfect. Meditation is a good way of understanding and improving your state of mind. The key is not to put yourself under pressure to be a perfect meditator. There is no such thing. Ideally, 10 minutes per day is an excellent start point, even doing this two to three times per week can make a real difference. There are many apps and courses available to learn about and start meditation. I have included some in the reference section at the end of the book (*see also* page 252).

You can also examine any unhelpful thinking styles such as:

- catastrophizing (what is the worst that can happen?)
- mental filter (only paying attention to certain types of evidence)
- personalization (is it really my fault, do I really have control over this?)
- jumping to conclusions through mind reading or fortune telling (what do I know for sure?)
- all-or-nothing thinking (maybe there is some grey here).

Finally, there is an exercise I use with clients called the AGA (Anxiety-Gratitude-Action) Exercise. Draw out three columns. In the left-hand column, write all the things that are causing you stress or anxiety – it may be a long list. In the second column, write next to the anxiety a reason to be grateful for that anxiety. This might seem counterintuitive but take for example the anxiety around caring for a sick parent. The gratitude column could be that you are glad they are still alive and that you get to spend time with them. The final column is the action you are going to take to tackle the anxiety.

Remember the distinction between worry (short-term and useful) and anxiety (long-term and unhelpful). This exercise will help break down the non-specific anxiety that you feel, reframe it and give you concrete actions to tackle it. Anxieties become worries when you attach an action to them.

If that doesn't appeal, then there is Jos Buttler's approach. A prolific international cricketer, he used to suffer terrible self-doubt, fear of failure and letting people down. One day he wrote 'Fuck it' on the top of his bat handle so that every time he looked down before facing the bowler he saw it – he had a hot run of form after that moment.

State-of-Mind Goals

What is one step you can take to work on your state of mind?

....

....

....

Pillar 2 – Sleep

One night of less than five hours' sleep, or two nights of less than seven hours' sleep. What do these nights have in common? They all lead to sleep deprivation, which in turn doubles the likelihood of death from ANY cause. Whether dying from a car accident, cancer, or a heart attack, sleep deprivation makes it twice as likely.

On a slightly less extreme note, sleep deprivation also causes emotional instability and cognitive impairment to the extent that driving when drowsy is as dangerous as drunk driving. Sleep is when we mentally and physically recuperate and re-energize. It allows us to deal with what has happened during the day, process events and feelings, and lay down memories.

Sleep is when we empty the stress bucket that has filled up during the day; it puts our body into repair mode. What happens when we have a poor night's sleep is that we start the next day with the stress bucket part-full. This means it fills up more quickly and then starts overflowing during the day. We know this feeling – it is one of irritability and anxiety, of feeling indecisive and below our best. We then try to sleep with a more agitated mind, sleep worse, become stressed about sleeping worse and the stress-sleep deprivation downward spiral is started.

Sleep is literally the foundation of a Maverick Life. Without it, we cannot tap the energy needed to create change, we do not have the energy to get things done or the desire to go out and deepen our key relationships.

There are tips that can help sleep, but first things first: the biggest root cause of poor sleep is stress. We've just looked at stress – reducing your stress levels is all but guaranteed to improve your sleep. Once you have begun to loosen the iron grip of stress there are some sleep tips universally agreed among the experts:

1) Wind down – starting two to three hours from when you want to fall asleep, begin to reduce the amount of emotional and mental stimulation.
2) Routine – create a regular pattern and timing in the run-up to going to sleep and in waking-up time. Sleeping in late at the weekend is sadly not helpful.
3) Nil by mouth – alcohol, nicotine, caffeine and food all make it harder to fall and stay asleep. Where possible, stick to water or herbal tea in the three hours before going to sleep. Try to avoid

alcohol and nicotine. Caffeine intake needs to stop six to seven hours before you head to sleep.

4) A dark room to fall asleep, a light room to wake up in. This helps the body recognize when to sleep. If you can, open the curtains before falling asleep, provided the room is dark. If not, it's best to leave them shut.
5) Expose yourself to natural sunlight. Artificial light messes up our cycles. Spend as much time outside as you can.
6) Have a hot bath. This increases relaxation and the temperature drop when you get out of the bath induces drowsiness.
7) Keep the room where you sleep at around 18 degrees – a hot room results in poor sleep.
8) Screens – contrary to popular belief, it is not the light from screens that damages sleep, it is the mental stimulation. Computers are worse than tablets, which are worse than TV, simply because of the level of engagement they create. Checking email or news during your two- to three-hour wind-down massively impacts your sleep. Keep screens out of the bedroom if the temptation is too much. Reading for pleasure is OK, but not reading for work, or for taking in information that could stimulate the brain. Many people do find that any type of blue light is not helpful and that red light or candlelight does help sleep as long as you remember to blow out the candle before sleep. You may need to buy an alarm clock if you currently use your phone for waking up.
9) Regular exercise helps, but not in the wind-down period.
10) Keep a notebook by your bed – that way, thoughts or worries can be noted down and dealt with the next day.

If you really cannot sleep, or wake up and cannot get back to sleep, it is worth setting a time limit, say 20 minutes. Then, if you are still awake, get up and do something relaxing.

Much of the above is based on an excellent lecture I attended in 2019 by Geoff Bird, a Professor of Neuroscience at Oxford University. At one point a rather desperate member of the audience asked, 'What can I do in the evenings then?' This is a particular problem for the 30 per cent of the population who are night owls and have their natural rhythm ruined by a morning-based society.

If you have a set time when you need to be up there really is no way around working backwards, allowing eight hours sleep and then two to three hours of pre-sleep relaxation. This means that if your alarm goes off at 7 a.m., then it is asleep at 11, no caffeine after 4 or 5 p.m. and decreasing mental or emotional stimulation from 8 or 9 p.m. Remember, socializing is mentally stimulating, so opt for an early dinner if you are with others.

I know the above can seem a long and rather daunting list and in places rather terrifying. My aim is not to increase your stress and thus contribute to less sleep. Can I ask you to accept the importance of sleep, work on reducing your stress levels and then adopt as many of the 10 steps listed above as you can? This is not an overnight fix, it may take months to reach a point of good sleep, but the journey is worth it.

Rest can certainly work alongside sleep; even warriors need to rest. We humans are designed for short, sharp bursts of activity. Think about school lessons of 30–50 minutes, which create spans of concentration followed by a rest. Building rest into your day, which can be sitting still or actively walking for example, can be highly effective in building productivity and raising good moods.

Many clients ask about sleep trackers. There are advanced trackers that fit on top of your mattress and can even moderate temperature. However, even relatively affordable ones like a Garmin watch or an Oura ring will gather a lot of information. The key is to use the information to slowly make changes, rather than become stressed in trying to chase a better sleep score instantly. For me, it highlighted the direct link between alcohol and poor sleep, which brings us neatly to the next pillar of self.

Good Sleep

What change will you make to improve your sleep and rest?

....

....

....

....

Pillar 3: Eating and Drinking

We are what we eat and you cannot exercise your way out of a bad diet. While we may intellectually know or understand that our diet is important, often we ignore it. After all, food and alcohol seem to make us feel better, they are comforting and in the short term seem to relieve anxiety and stress. But look at it this way: have you ever filled a diesel car with petrol? I did once. We drove away from the petrol station, everything was fine for about two miles, then very quickly we ground to a halt. Six hours later, we were back on the road, lesson learnt.

It matters what fuel you put in the car and in the same way, it matters what fuel you put in your body. Although we seem to be able to cope with a wide variety of food, the reality is that on an individual and population basis what we consume has a major impact on our health, our state of mind and our energy levels.

There is no replacement for moderation in eating and drinking. The Japanese have a concept of stopping eating when you are 80 per cent full as there is a 20-minute delay in the stomach getting the message through to the brain to stop eating. This is why most of us like to bolt our food before our brains can tell us to stop. The idea of binge eating and then binge dieting just does not work. Instead, developing a pattern of eating and drinking during the week that works for you is key. The magic spot is a good amount of exercise (more in the next section) and a balanced healthy diet, with of course the occasional blowout – let's not rob food of all pleasure and enjoyment.

Snacking can be a problem depending on why you are doing it. If you are genuinely hungry, then eating a high-fibre snack between meals is not a problem. However, if you are an emotional eater (yes, I am one) then unhealthy snacks eaten to alleviate boredom or make you feel better are likely to lead to weight gain and health problems.

The research around the health of our guts is exploding. Our microbiome, which consists of trillions of microorganisms or microbes, plays many key roles in supporting the effective daily operation of the body. These microbes include bacteria, fungi, parasites and viruses, many of which are located in the gut. Our gut microbiome is particularly linked to the immune system and tissue regeneration. Increasingly, the state and balance of our microbiome is being linked to our mental health. Our diet has a direct impact on the composition of our microbiome.

Here are some key principles to observe with food:

1) Fresh is best, eat organic where possible.
2) Moderation – you can't be 'perfect' all the time.
3) Eat less meat; use meat as flavouring or as a side dish.
4) Eat a wide variety of plant-based food – eat the rainbow (food of all colours) to ensure a good mix of minerals and vitamins.
5) Avoid all ultra-processed food, e.g. food that no longer resembles the original ingredient or has chemical additives.
6) Count chemicals rather than calories. Eat food that looks like food rather then something made in a factory with a long list of ingredients.

7) Cut back on added and refined sugars (e.g. table sugar or sugars that have been extracted from food and made into flavourings or sweeteners).
8) Drink more water instead of caffeine (two litres of water per day and if you do drink caffeine then a maximum of four cups of coffee or five cups of tea).
9) Consume less processed salt.
10) Include fermented products such as kefir, kombucha and kimchi in your diet to enrich the gut microbiome.
11) Plan snacks, one to two per day, and in amounts that alleviate hunger rather than replace your next meal. Where possible, snack on raw veg and nuts.
12) Find a system that works for you. Try intermittent fasting – the 5:2 diet can be particularly effective – or create eating windows, say 12–8 p.m. This gives your gut a break and can aid weight loss, and is beneficial for long-term health.
13) Plan ahead and be careful when travelling or away from home. Grab-and-go food and snacks are often ultra-processed.

Alcohol

I once heard a client say, 'I don't drink if I have to work the next day', which is a pretty good maxim for life. Alcohol, apart from being a poison and a depressant, has a major impact on your performance and mood over the following hours and days. The problem is that drinking is so pervasive in most societies. You hear DJs on the radio saying things like, 'You've earned yourself a drink tonight', or you turn on the TV and there are likely to be scenes of drinking everywhere. I remember going to a pantomime one year with our small children and Father Christmas was drinking during and after his all-nighter. No wonder then that we assume it is normal and acceptable.

It is worth a quick check on what the current recommended limits are based on extensive research:

In the US

Fourteen standard drinks per week – no more than four in any one night. A standard drink defined as a bottle of beer (350ml), two-thirds of a pint, a small glass of wine (150ml), a shot of spirits.

Roughly eight pints or two and a half bottles of wine or half a bottle of spirits per week.

In the UK

Fourteen units per week, spread over at least three days. Units are roughly half a pint, half a standard glass of wine or one small shot of spirits.

Six pints or one and a half bottles of wine, a third of a bottle of spirits per week.

How does your intake compare? Do you keep a track of it? If not, there are lots of apps you can use, or a note on your phone. I used to drink a fair amount mainly to self soothe and deal with stress or to relax in social situations. I would find myself wincing when asked on health questionnaires how many units I consumed every week. Like many of us, I suspect, I rounded down. For years I wanted to drink less, but it had become my reward, my way of winding down at the end of a stressful day. Looking back, I realize that I could have worked to make the days less stressful but instead I had established a dangerous habit.

I began to make changes slowly. It was easy to swap beer for non-alcoholic beer most nights; a cold can of beer still feels like a good way to end the day, with or without alcohol. The major change came when I bought a Garmin watch that measured my sleep. The impact of alcohol was startling. Although I felt like I was sleeping after a few drinks, my watch showed that I was never entering a proper deep sleep. I was not recovering and crucially my body was not able to do the mental or physical repair work needed to start the next day in good shape. Every morning the watch gave me a sleep score out of 100. I noticed that even after one or two drinks my sleep score was at least 20 points less than normal. Over a few days that added up to exhaustion and low mood, which in turn led to lower productivity and further low mood.

Drinking less and less made me see how much more energy I had, how much more curious I was in the world. I write this now still wanting to quit completely but not quite there yet. I am, however, thrilled to have developed a system and awareness that means I can now fill in those forms without wincing, answering within the recommended limits. It is no coincidence that the completion of this book coincided with a big drop in alcohol intake. Try it.

We often use food and alcohol as a form of self-medication. Comfort eating or excessive drinking can feel like they are numbing or reducing painful feelings, only for those feelings to return stronger the next day. Think about why you are over-consuming. Are you eating and drinking alone a lot? They are both social activities, easing and strengthening relationships when used reasonably in this way. If you find yourself overdoing it then you may have found ways by yourself or with certain others of justifying this. Use this book to look at what you might be seeking comfort from and try to work on the root cause.

You can revisit the work you did on your void (*see* pages 18–19). We all have some sense of emptiness, and experience phases of loss of meaning. We can turn to food and alcohol to try and ease these feelings, but a better solution is to accept these feelings as human and work on more positive interventions when we feel like this.

Alcohol

What is your plan to work on what and why you consume? Write out the key action here:

....

....

....

....

Pillar 4: Exercise

Exercise in whatever form you prefer – or is least unpleasant – is one of the key underpinnings of a happy, healthy life. Some of us can do all forms of exercise and for others this will be limited. It does not matter what form of exercise you are taking, if you are able to establish a regular routine and to elevate the heart rate and use the lungs. The dull-looking chart that follows is what has given me the motivation to exercise over the 15 years since I first saw it:

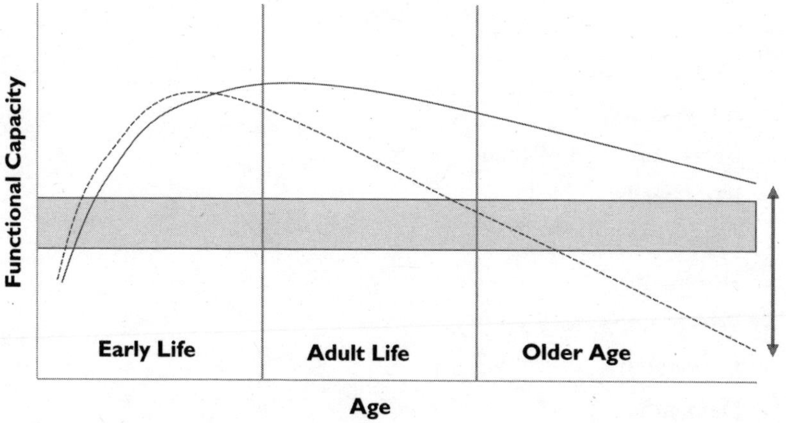

Functional capacity, on the left-hand axis, is defined as an ability to go about normal life – to work, to lift up your children, to drive and to play sport. It is also a proven predictor of cardiac health. Above the threshold is the range for people to maintain a normally active life. Below the threshold shaded in grey and you are classified as incapacitated. Age is the axis along the bottom of the chart.

The two curves represent two approaches to lifestyle:

1) The dotted curve shows a sedentary lifestyle with a poor diet. This shows that the person never reaches 100 per cent of their potential capacity and is incapacitated by the age of 50, with a life expectancy of 55.
2) The solid curve shows someone who eats well and takes regular exercise (normally defined as 30 minutes at least three times per week). In this case, 100 per cent capacity is reached at 15, but the crucial difference is that this person never drops below 50 per cent capacity until their death on average at 90. That means, in theory, being able to lead a normal active life throughout a long life.

If that is not enough motivation, according to the National Health Service in the UK it is medically proven that people who do regular physical activity have a lower risk of:

- Coronary heart disease and stroke
- Type 2 diabetes
- Bowel cancer
- Breast cancer in women
- Early death
- Osteoarthritis
- Hip fracture
- Falls (among older adults)
- Depression
- Dementia.

Other studies also find a boost to your libido and better quality sleep.

If that encourages you to start thinking about exercising more regularly, here are 10 ideas that have really helped my clients exercise more and reach the solid curve in the chart above:

1) Involve someone else whenever possible – not only does this make it more fun, it also makes it much more likely that you will turn up and exercise.
2) Three times a week is a minimum – tempting though it is to do one long run a week, the research shows that three x 30 minutes of exercise is the minimum to reach the solid curve. If you are unable to run, vigorous walks have been seen to have the same impact as swimming. Find something that you can do and build up slowly from your current levels. Try not to increase time or distance by more than 10 per cent per week or two.
3) Always have a goal – preferably an external goal, with internal benefits coming as a by-product. Internal goals such as losing weight or improving your health are great, but are easy to talk yourself out of on a dark February night. Not so easy is the event that you have entered (a couple per year seems to work); even more if you have entered with friends or are raising money for charity.
4) Find something that you enjoy doing – for at least two of the three sessions. If you hate running and set up a programme involving running three times a week, even with the chart in mind you are never going to keep it up. Write a long list with two columns – 'exercise I enjoy' and 'exercise I do not'. Think creatively, it does not have to be about lifting weights in the gym. The research shows that a brisk 30-minute walk is enough. A quick round of golf, playing squash with a friend, walking the dog… all these can count towards your three-a-week. It is no coincidence that dog owners live longer and are happier.

5) Track your progress – for some people it is deeply satisfying seeing their fitness improve and keeping a log of what they have done, like keeping a diary, greatly increases the chances of continuing. There are many brilliant smartphone apps now (Strava being one of the most popular), or go old school and start a logbook.
6) Build exercise into your diary and routine – it just does not work getting to the end of the day or week and thinking, *oh, I suppose I have to go out for a run*. You will not do it; no one is that good at motivating themselves on the spot. I am a great believer in routine as it creates habit and it also lets everyone else (partner, kids, friends) know when you are not around. Find three (preferably four) slots in the week that work for you, block them out as repeating events in your diary and then at the start of each week figure out which ones work for you that week.
7) Be outdoors for at least two of the sessions – nature is a huge natural stimulant. Pounding away in the gym is just not the same and running repeatedly on a treadmill, for example, can create problems with feet, knees and hips. Find a route or a landscape that you love, even if it means driving or cycling a little way first.
8) Mix it up – have a range of sports/exercise you enjoy doing. Doing the same thing repeatedly even in the most motivated of us will lead to boredom and possible injury. Even professional athletes cross-train. Go back to the list from point 4 and make sure you have captured everything you have ever tried.
9) Try something new and then add to that list things you have not tried but would love to. Find out how to start street dancing, paddle boarding, garden or trail walk – go on, google it and sign up now!
10) Be kind to yourself – this is not easy; it requires real motivation and self-discipline. If you have a week where you only exercise twice, don't get annoyed with yourself. If the majority of weeks see three sessions of exercise, you are well on your way to the solid curve.

Exercise

What is your next step towards developing an exercise plan that works for you?

....

....

....

....

In Summary

My summary of this chapter...

1. ....

2. ....

3. ....

Key Points

1. We create unnecessary stress in our lives. Reducing this can have a huge impact on our effectiveness and state of mind.

2. We need to combine mental and physical approaches, the mind and body are inseparable.

3. Creating a routine that works for us around sleep, exercise and nutrition is the starting point.

CHAPTER ELEVEN

Others

A few years ago, we took my brother-in-law gliding for his 50th birthday. This was a world with which I was completely unfamiliar. We entered a warm group of around 50 regulars. Norms and behaviours were well established, from who sat where to who helped who up into the sky. Everyone had their role and the day ran at a relaxed but purposeful pace. I was both enamoured by the gliders (and the gliding) and at the same time somewhat envious. They seemed so comfortable and secure in their group with their shared mission. It set me thinking – do we all need more of a clan?

Bees need a hive as we humans need a clan. Historically, we survived not by being the biggest but by banding together. It seems in today's world we are doing the opposite, whether at an international level, a national level or even at street level. Communities are harder to come by and are perhaps seen as something 'older' people do. One of the reasons the Danes are so happy (regularly topping polls) is the high percentage of them that live in communes. Often, they cook once a month for 100 people. So why don't we all live in communes, helping each other every day?

There is a fascinating study from 2015 by Dr Brett Ford at Berkeley University into how culture impacts the pursuit of happiness. He looked at what happened when people decided that they wanted to become happier. In all the countries he studied, except the US, people were able to make themselves happier. The key difference is that their view of happiness was collective, so they became happier by doing something for someone else. In the US, which is essentially an individualistic culture, they found that trying to become happier by doing something for yourself does not work.

The irony is that we live in a world where self-care is a serious concept and the idea of taking time out to meditate or have a hot bath is seen as a cure-all. This misses the point; it is the pace and intensity of the rest of our day that is the problem. Self-care in isolation will not make us happier, as we are not helping our clan. Being part of a clan also helps with accountability – a key Maverick underpinning. We will look more closely at this in Chapter 13.

Loneliness

In the US, they have been running a survey for several years – how many friends could you call on in a crisis? Twenty years ago, the most common answer was five, today it is zero. Loneliness is an increasing problem in the Western world and is linked to depression and other health issues such as anxiety. Anxiety can be directly tracked through measuring micro-waking – those times in the night when we wake and go back to sleep. Measured as typically high in the Western world, in remote clans, despite the inherent danger levels being higher, micro waking is almost non-existent. The clan creates a sense of safety and reduces anxiety.

Remember the Grant Study at Harvard in Chapter 6 (see also page 60)? The unequivocal finding was that the strength of your relationships is a key factor in mental and physical health. 'Loneliness has the same impact on mortality as smoking 15 cigarettes a day, making it even more dangerous than obesity,' said Douglas Nemecek MD, Chief Medical Officer for Behavioural Health at the insurer Cigna. A decreasing circle of friends really can be a death sentence.

Loneliness is not the same as social isolation. It is quite possible to be lonely in a city where you interact with many people each day. It is not the interaction that prevents loneliness, it is having a reciprocal relationship with someone, involving mutual aid. This explains how it is very possible to be lonely in a marriage even if you see your partner every day. Increasingly, loneliness is even seen as a major contributor to addiction. Professor Bruce Alexander has done some fascinating studies in his 'rat park'. If you put a single rat in a small cage with two bottles, one containing water, the other water and heroin, the rat will quickly become addicted to the heroin water. However, if you create a 'rat park' where there are other rats, obstacles and play objects, with the same two bottles, the rats almost never drink the heroin water.

Hilary Cash runs an internet rehab centre, focused on gamers. She points out that one of the reasons why games can be so addictive (deliberately) is that they fulfil many basic psychological needs no longer met by society. She gives examples of belonging to a group, having a sense of identity and a chance to have status and rise in status. Gaming does not ease loneliness though as in an online community it is harder to create a deeper sense of connection.

Really belonging and feeling part of something is different to trying to fit in. Fitting in is tiring – you are bending yourself somehow, being someone you are not. Belonging is where you are true to yourself, you can relax and feel loved and seen.

So perhaps being part of a clan really does help with well-being. Have a think about your clan. Do you see enough of them? Do you have a clan, or do you need to find one? If work is your main clan, perhaps it is time to look outside of this for a more harmonious life.

Go back to the constellation you created in Chapter 3 (*see also* page 27). Are there enough people on there, are the relationships in good enough shape? How do you feel differently now? Epictetus, a Greek Stoic philosopher, is quoted as saying, 'The key is to keep company only with people who uplift you, whose presence calls forth your best.'

Communication

The Modern Maverick may live outside of the generic expectations of society, but that does not mean living in isolation or alone. We cannot create a meaningful life with a positive contribution on our own. If we accept that relationships are key to a Maverick Life, what are the basic tenets of good relationships? When you read books and listen to talks on the subject, most point to the central importance of good communication.

Emily and Laurence Alison are forensic psychologists who specialize in criminal interrogations. In their book *Rapport: The Four Ways to Read People*, they outline the best way to create rapport and good communication. Rapport has four key elements – with the acronym, HEAR:

1) Honesty – be objective and direct when communicating your feelings or intentions. Note that complete bluntness is *not* what this is. The Chinese have an expression, 'Do not use a hatchet to remove a fly from your friend's forehead'.
2) Empathy – understand someone based on recognition of their core beliefs and values, which will be different from yours. Listen from both your heart and mind. Tune into tone/pace/body movements, not just the words. Forget trying to prepare your next point or comparing what they are saying to your own experiences. You are listening for the speaker's intent and feelings.
3) Autonomy – empathize with other people's free will and right to choose whether to co-operate in what they tell you. No coercion or manipulation, they must want to talk to you.
4) Reflection – identify and repeat back those elements that are significant, meaningful and tactical to help guide a conversation towards the goal.

You know when you are really being listened to; it is a magical and rare experience. The listener has temporarily put their ego aside and you are the centre of attention. Suspending the chatter in your head requires practice. Defer judgement and offer opinions carefully, having asked permission to do so. Curiosity and compassion make for better conversations and relationships than judgements. You will know when you are being listened to properly – the person in front of you will light up. Here are some communication fundamentals that apply to all the next sections:

- think clearly about what needs to be said (key messages)
- work out the best way of saying something (careful choice of words)
- think about the style of conversation (tone)
- identify who is best to say what
- create the right environment to chat (setting)
- know when best to have that chat (right time, right mood, etc.)
- find a comfortable way to start/finish the conversation
- check what has been heard and understood. If necessary, ask the person to write out a summary, or check in again in the next few days
- if anyone becomes emotional or triggered, take a break. Walk for a few minutes, take some deep breaths. When our flight-or-fight system is triggered, our brains are incapable of constructive or useful conversations.

Pillar 5: Partner

With roughly 40–50 per cent of marriages ending in divorce (depending on where you live), there are clearly many pitfalls on the way to a long-term romantic partnership. These can include young children, teenagers, ageing parents, health issues, careers to be managed, money to be made, different values and so on. The inside of a partnership is a constantly shifting vortex, often struggling to stay resilient as storms rage around it. If you are currently between partners, or if a romantic partner is not something you want out of life, then this section is still relevant as many of the ideas can be applied to friendships and family relationships as well.

Left alone, a relationship has entropy – the batteries discharge and one day you look at each other and there is an empty space, with nothing left to salvage (nor the will to do so). Much like a garden will return to the wild when left untended, so too a partnership will lessen and separate unless care and attention is taken. I have worked with many clients who focus too much on their businesses or careers only to find their partners suddenly delivering an ultimatum.

Many couples I have seen have had to go and stand at the edge of the cliff, acknowledging the parlous state of their relationship. At this point some jump and separate, while others turn back, redoubling efforts. The prospect of being alone, of co-parenting, of financial diminution, of not having tried hard enough is often enough to break the downward cycle. Success at this point often involves a good relationship therapist who can point out harmful behaviour and create a space for honest conversation and improved communication.

The other key role of a therapist is to point out the familiar scripts and dialogues that exist in every relationship. The dance often begins with a sharp comment from one side and a standard riposte from the other then kicks off the familiar verbal boxing match. Each time this is repeated, the stuck record is grooved further. Breaking out of these word tussles is key to developing and deepening a relationship.

Jim had a successful business and a life that from the outside looked rosy. Three young kids, a large extended family and work that was meaningful. Underneath this external image, however, his marriage was in trouble. He felt attacked and unsupported, his wife felt that he was not doing enough and they could not find a way to talk about it.

As a family they were under a huge amount of pressure. Health issues with their children, parents ill and dying, all against the backdrop of a full and demanding work life for both of them.

His wife was reluctant to engage in therapy. She carried some difficult past experiences with her and to open the door to examining this was a very big step. Through coaching, though, she began to see that there were safe, non-threatening ways of having good, honest conversations.

They reached an end point where both were planning how a separation would work. At some point, as they were contemplating the real possibility of splitting up, a renewed commitment arose in both of them. They found a good therapist who they trusted and the conversations were hard but became warmer and kinder. Through this work, they were able to see how much they were both contributing to the family and how hard life would be if they were apart. The work continues, but a new path has opened up.

What are the steps back from the cliff edge? Turning away from the impact of separation is one, but what might you turn towards instead? The glow that surrounds a healthy, functioning relationship is created by both people being comfortable with themselves and being themselves in front of the other. This can only be achieved through honesty and vulnerability; it is counter-intuitive.

We may feel that we need to show ourselves to be strong or capable to our partners, when in fact the path to a meaningful relationship is to be ourselves, our fragile complicated and confused selves, in all our glory and insecurity. You can start with something small, a revelation about how you are feeling, or a more honest answer to a gentle question. Perhaps make a small act of kindness; a cup of tea or a piece of toast. Anything that is out of the ordinary, that breaks the established pattern.

In their excellent and simple book *What Mums Want and Dads Need to Know*, Harry and Kate Benson describe three wants:

1) Be a friend – doing things as a couple and spending time together
2) Be interested in me
3) Be interested in the children.

This does not sound too hard. However, it does point to the non-Maverick heart of the problem, which is an over-prioritization of work. We cannot manage the three simple acts listed above if we are preoccupied and exhausted by our work. Our partners tend to get the dregs of us when really they deserve the best of us. Spending time together away from the energy drains (work, children, life) is key. Time away together, even a couple of nights, can have a major impact on recharging the love battery.

Kate and Harry go on to describe the four relationship wreckers – STOP for short:

- **S**coring points
- **T**hinking the worst
- **O**pting out
- **P**utting down.

This also speaks to the original research by John Gottman, famed for his work on marital stability and divorce. He named the magic ratio of 5:1. For every negative interaction during moments of conflict a happy marriage has at least five positive interactions. That is a big ratio. So how can we show appreciation and love for our partners?

The author of *The 5 Love Languages*, Gary Chapman, thinks that we mostly go wrong because we do not understand our partner's language of love. We need to know how they best hear the love and appreciation we need to express. He talks about five very different languages:

1) Time
2) Words
3) Actions
4) Gifts
5) Touch

Assuming your partner speaks the same language as you is problematic. Ask them, or even better try and guess each other's and then ask for the right answer. You may not know your own language, but some joint thinking will uncover it.

Partner

What is your first action to improve the relationship with your partner?

....

....

....

....

Pillar 6: Kids

We tend to be tyrannized by inbound demands on our time. Whether via our inboxes or phones, or addictive social media and news, our attention and effort are sucked into a seemingly endless stream of top priority actions. In contrast, our children are less adept at making their needs known and unmet needs are often expressed through seemingly unconnected poor behaviour.

In business, we are taught to distinguish between urgent and important, learning to focus on the latter. While parenting is not the most urgent thing we do, there is no doubt that for the parents of the world, it is the most important. Fifty per cent of our 'set' happiness levels in life is determined by our genes and upbringing. The issue for our 'instant gratification' society is that the impact of parenting can take five, 10, 15 or even 50 years to show up. Our childhood casts long shadows.

As parents, we feel great pressure. This pressure is further intensified by an increasingly competitive school and graduate job scene and a fear of dire consequences if grades are not achieved. At the same time, we rarely receive or even seek help or training in the parenting arena and it is taboo to offer advice. We might study for years to become a doctor or read endless books about our hobbies, but how much time do we spend learning to be parents? Society expects us to be born perfect parents. What can we do?

First, we need to commit. This might sound strange because of course we are committed parents. Commitment is not just about time, it is around the priority we allocate to our kids, particularly in the crucial first 12 years of their development. Doing what we can to produce happy prosocial children who can go on to become balanced and economically productive adults will be the most meaningful thing we do. They literally carry us forward to future generations. The small things that we do repeatedly every day add up.

For most of us this probably means spending more time at 'home'. Steve Biddulph, a leading child psychologist, wrote in his book, *Raising Boys*: 'If you routinely work a 55- or 60-hour week, including travel times, you just won't cut it as a dad.'

Jess had started her own business that had grown to several members of staff. She felt she needed to be there all the time, to set a good example. She began to see that her skills and contribution were more outside the business, meeting potential clients, thinking about strategy, finding out what was going on in the industry. She also began to realize that she was not seeing her family or her friends enough – she had channelled everything into the first years of the business.

She gave herself permission to be out of the office more. Some of this time she used for work, but a few times a week she would leave home later or meet a friend for lunch. Her energy levels increased, she felt better and her impact on the business went up. Everyone benefitted.

We also need to accept that we will not get it right all the time. We can, however, get it very wrong and that has lasting impact on our children's lives. We need to ensure they do not have Adverse Childhood Experiences (ACEs). These include emotional, physical or sexual abuse, emotional neglect, substance abuse, parental separation or divorce. Sixty-seven per cent of us have at least one of these ACEs. Four or more means you are 11 times more likely to abuse drugs, or 4.5 times more likely to develop depression.

If we can avoid ACEs, what do we need to focus on? In the landmark British Cohort Study, where people are followed over 50 years, Professor Richard Layard at LSE finds three traits in children that predict fulfilment later in life. They are in order of importance:

1) Emotional health
2) Social behaviour
3) Academic achievement.

The study suggests a shift in focus of our parenting input, perhaps less around achievement and school to more about creating a holding environment at home where our kids can flourish emotionally and socially. Interestingly, in the same study family income only accounted for 0.5 per cent of the variation in life satisfaction in later adult life. The non-Maverick is over-focused on the material side of a child's life: big house, nice holidays. It turns out what children really want is your time and attention, not your money.

There are many different models of parenting and often advice is conflicting. There are times when we feel like we do not know what we are doing and long periods where we may feel disconnected from our children (and ourselves). We will choose our own style and approach, but are there any useful universal truths?

From reading around the literature, there seem to be two key aspects of good parenting: modelling and communication. These both start with making time and paying attention. In terms of modelling, it seems that being fair, consistent and following through are good places to start. Also, being aware of quite how sponge-like children are in observing and processing your actions and emotions. Living a Maverick Life is a good modelling exercise.

Communication is a theme that runs through almost all of parenting literature, so how do we talk more effectively to our children? Parent educator and author Steve Biddulph proposes the importance of making 'time to talk'. His ideas for how to talk centre around listening with full attention and the importance of opportunities such as car journeys for both talking and spending time in stillness. He speaks about trying to be light-hearted and limiting the number of questions asked so that children do not feel interrogated – for example, instead of 'how was your day today?,' try, 'It's lovely to have you home' when your children return from school. He speaks, too, about the importance of acknowledging and naming your child's feelings.

I often ask clients what sort of parent they want to be and they nearly all reply 'present'. If I had to pick one theme for us as parents, apart from not pretending that any of us know what we are doing, it would be the words of one frustrated head teacher, who posted this sign at the school gate: 'Greet your children with a smile, not a phone'.

So, from reviewing both Richard Layard's findings and work by Martin Seligman in the field of positive psychology, there seem to be three core skills to help our children develop happy and fulfilled lives, assuming that academic achievement is mainly taken care of at school:

- resilience
- self-belief
- strong relationships.

Resilience is built around the importance of stretching, risk taking and making mistakes. Being open as parents about the mistakes you make, and accepting constructive criticism, can help you have open conversations when your children make mistakes. We simply cannot grow or learn without making mistakes – watch a toddler at work.

Self-belief centres around recognizing the individual in your child, the early Maverick, and celebrating their spark. Encourage them to use this spark by creating opportunities for it and building a storehouse of special moments when they have come alive and triumphed. Building autonomy through listening rather than solving, not ascribing 'roles', and use of descriptive praise of effort and activity rather than achievement is key. In the same way you are learning as a Maverick to ignore the 'should', watch what expectations you place on your children.

Empower them through involving them in family decisions and tasks, reminding them that they always have a choice in how to behave or act. Having a strong family identity with clear values and a strong sense of belonging also helps. Kids 'overhear' everything, so allow them to hear you praising them to another adult.

For strong relationships the first port of call is to look at the space between you and your partner. This is what your children will model from. Is there (mostly) mutual respect in place, open communication, open disagreement and resolution? Do they see you go through the cycle of rupture and repair – arguing and then making up? Have you created a positive 'holding environment' at home? Are you 'joined up' in the way you parent? Talking about your feelings, and how your children's behaviour makes you feel, is also important.

Separating their behaviour from their character can lead to breakthroughs here: it's crucial not to label your children as 'bad' when you mean that their behaviour is inappropriate. Having an open house where your friends and their friends can come and go helps build strong relationships. The final part of building strong relationships is stating clear expectations with clear consequences for misbehaviour.

One of the most trusted parenting books is written by Adele Faber and Elaine Mazlish. Called *How to Talk so Kids will Listen and Listen so Kids will Talk*, they highlight six key points:

1) Help your children with feelings; listen with full attention and acknowledge their feelings with a word – 'Oh, I see', don't necessarily agree. Help them name their feelings and resist trying to make it better or give advice. Sometimes you just need to mirror and acknowledge their feelings.
2) Engage co-operation; describe what you see or the problem – 'What a mess'. Talk about how it makes you feel. Try writing a note or using one word – 'Bath!' Try for the overall attitude of you are basically a loveable capable person, right now there is a problem that needs attention – be honest.
3) Non-punishment – experience consequences of misbehaviour but not as punishment. Express your feelings strongly without attacking character, 'I am furious that you left my saw outside'. State your expectations – tools should be returned – and show how to make amends. Give them a choice: borrow and return or give up borrowing altogether. If you need to do so, lock the toolbox. Try problem solving together – what would their solution be?
4) Encourage autonomy – let kids make choices. Show respect for their struggle. Talk about dreams and aspirations without taking away hope. Don't rush to answer questions or take over, ask them how they feel.
5) Praise – instead of evaluating describe, let them evaluate and self-praise. Describe what you see, what you feel. Sum up the praiseworthy behaviour in a word. Avoid 'I knew you could do it', accept distress in failure, avoid excessive enthusiasm.
6) No role playing – e.g. 'You are the clumsy one'. Look for opportunities to show a new picture. Let them overhear you say positive things and model behaviour you would like to see. Help them create a storehouse for special moments.

As a final round-up, this was a summary of a panel about parenting teenagers at a local school with a mix of parents and teachers:

1) Pick your battles
2) Be aware of monthly hormonal cycles and make allowances
3) You are not there to be their friend, boundaries are key
4) Your teenage years were not the same, do not compare
5) Empower and encourage grit, involve them in decisions, explain short-term pain for long-term gain
6) You are a role model, act as one
7) Trust them, but expect them to make mistakes
8) Discipline is key, overcome being scared to parent
9) Don't try to fix everything for them
10) Trust your instinct – if something doesn't feel right, it probably isn't.

If you would like more information, The Common Sense Media website is a good place to start (www.commonsensemedia.org). Also the resources section at www.teentips.co.uk.

Kids

What is the first action to work on your relationship with your children?

....

....

....

....

Pillar 7: Friends and family

'If you want to change the world, go home and love your family.' I saw this quote, usually attributed to Mother Teresa, on a wall in a shop called Family and it gnawed away at me for weeks. But why? The current state of the world is well-documented, everyone I speak to wishes they could do more and at the same time is lost about how to, so we tend to give up. But that does not sit so well with us; we want to help, to make things better. Does this quote give us an opening, a direction where we could channel our time and energy?

What sits at the heart of this idea is that our greatest impact starts at a very local, personal level. This seems very at odds with the non-Maverick modern definition of success through impact and recognition away from our communities. One of the products of technology has been a widening of our unit of reference and outlook, from our home and community to the entire planet. We feel that we are not really having an impact unless we are helping many people. It is this idea that is so disempowering, that somehow being local is not enough.

Mother Teresa took a different view. The quote at the beginning of this section came from an interview in 1972 after she had won the Nobel Peace Prize. She was asked, 'What can we do to promote world peace?' Her answer was the quote above. She went on to say, 'Spread love everywhere you go: first of all in your own house. Give love to your children, to your wife or husband, to a next-door neighbour… let no one ever come to you without leaving happier.'

Let's take a broad view of 'home' and 'family'. For some this will mean a nuclear family under the same roof, while for others, home may be several safe and welcoming places and family may be a group or clan that is not dictated by biology. What is clear to me, though, is that changing the world starts with those closest to you.

Imagine building a skyscraper: the foundations are critical and take months or years to build, during which time visible progress on the site is limited. It is only when the foundations are solid and in place that the building can rapidly rise from the ground. Your family are these foundations. With your time and love, they can go out into the world alongside you and bring about real change. You have multiplied your impact. Life starts and ends at home, not at work.

While most of us know that we need to be more present at home or in our community, life gets in the way. Work, travel, health… all seem to make demands of us that trump the quieter requests from nearer home. This does not always need to be a radical overhaul. I have seen clients and friends make major improvements to their relationships and impact on the world by adding a small amount of space and time at home, perhaps just once or twice a week.

How then do we love? What do we do with this extra time we have created at home and how do we make better use of the time we have already? It starts with connecting. Connecting means putting your phone down as you come into the house, it means turning your face and body towards the person you are talking to, taking a genuine interest in how they are and what is on their mind. Connecting means anticipating and understanding others' needs, often when they are not aware of those needs themselves. This may be when all you want is to come home and collapse. But if your day and your work colleagues have had the best of you, how can you change the world when you go home?

As you reflect where you spend your time and energy, remember that global success without local success is no success. Let's return to one of Bronnie Ware's five regrets of the dying (*see also* page 59). Number four was 'I wish I had stayed in touch with my friends'.

This really means old friends, those who have known you through a succession of ups and downs. They may have changed, they may not have, but there is a premium on a long friendship. That knowledge of another person gives you a level of richness in a relationship that is rare.

Of course, they will infuriate you and of course, they will frustrate you, but on some level there is a connection. Maybe they make you laugh, maybe they make you feel good, or maybe you help them in some way. They call you out if you are not being yourself or seem unhappy. It is easy to dismiss old friends sometimes and only when it is too late do you realize you wish you had stayed in touch.

There can be periods of estrangement with close friends and family. A remark is made that causes offence or is misinterpreted. Clumsy attempts to patch things up make it worse. Hiding behind intentions does not work: 'I did not mean to…' The point is you have caused hurt, whether intentional or not, whether you feel that they are being overly sensitive or not. There is immense pain in living estranged. Although it might feel like the easiest route to remove someone from your life, much like a phantom limb, they are always there.

Estrangement can be helpful in the short term if it means removing yourself from abusive or damaging behaviour. There is however sometimes a cost to estrangement: we leave some of our heart, our spirit with the other person. Consider whether the estrangement is helping you overall. If you would like to rebuild the relationship, then an honest heartfelt apology is often the starting point. Once you realize there is no right or wrong, no actual truth, more each person's own valid version of truth, then it becomes easier to see things from the other side. Acknowledging and recognizing their 'truth' opens a different conversation.

At our best it is hard to see or experience what it is like to be someone else. We look at everything through our own lens, even when we are trying to put ourselves in the other's shoes. When we are hurt, or triggered into child mode, it becomes impossible to even try to see how things look from the other viewpoint. Being aware of this, taking a break and practising curiosity and listening is a good starting point.

A client was having a difficult period with their sister. They had been close for a long time. They had said something that had caused her great hurt. They felt of course that they were in the right, that she was being sensitive. Often when you hurt someone, you have hit a nerve and that doesn't mean you are right or that your intention was a good one.

The pain though of not being on good terms, exacerbated by the need to speak about another family matter on a near-daily basis, became almost unbearable. Finally, late one night, the client realized they had reached the fork in the road. One direction led to permanent damage, the other to the chance of rebuilding the relationship. It was not clear which path to take at the time. They were upset, angry and of course convinced they were right.

It took a late night of reflection and recollection of an intervention from a friend to realize that what mattered more to them was the relationship than their hurt ego. They felt very liberated after giving a genuine apology the next morning and so began a six-month reconciliation process. The relationship is now stronger than ever and has gone from a huge psychological drain to a deep well of strength for both of them.

Who are you going to apologize to?

What role do we take in helping and protecting our close friends and family? When a friend committed suicide in 2018, I found myself asking this particular question. Although after reading and talking with others I realized that I could not have helped him, or changed his actions, all of us in his circle of friends were deeply shaken by it.

We resolved to form a friendship pledge. Each of us would have one close friend in mind, who we felt was in need. We would check in with them weekly and unless told not to do so by them, ask questions and push to find out how they were doing. When we are depressed, often we do not want to see or talk to others and push people away in the mistaken belief that we are poor company. Friends and family rise above that.

Who is your friend in need?

Writing this, I recognize that this is all fine in theory but how can we put it into practice? We know deep down that our relationships matter and we know we could do better so what stops us? I hope some of the ideas and stories in this chapter have helped increase your own awareness and that some will resonate with you. We will weave these into a plan in Chapter 13 and so for now, jot some thoughts down, reflect and discuss some of the ideas and be interested as to what emerges for you.

Friends and Family

The one relationship I am going to really focus on is with…

....

....

....

....

Pillar 8: Community and Planet

We have looked at operating at a very local level, friends and family. Is that enough? It is certainly the most important and if it is the focus of what we do for short periods of time then that is enough. However, at certain periods in our life we may have time and energy to look beyond that to our local communities and importantly beyond that to our global community.

In an age when we move away from our families and travel to work, we tend not to build ties in our communities. This causes problems. Those in need are not helped, communities splinter into factions and the social fabric frays. Giving time to your community is important (*see also* Chapter 12, pages 173–6 for more details).

There is also a broader sense of community and that is humankind. For the first time in our history, we face a truly global threat, of global warming. One that requires concerted action at an individual, community, business, government and global level. Deciding where you can have the most impact is crucial.

This can feel totally overwhelming. Many people turn away from it. We need to come together as a collective of individuals and achieve the changes required. The Modern Maverick recognizes the importance of helping on the biggest problems we face rather than just lining our own nests.

As individuals, we can create a planet plan at three different levels:

- Our home – we can understand our carbon footprint. You can do this at calculators such as www.carbonfootprint.com. As a first step we can offset this; for a typical household, at the time of writing this might cost £100 per annum. This is however only a short-term solution. We need to plan what steps we are taking as individuals and a family to get to carbon zero or even better, carbon negative. A useful source of information is the meta study in 2020 by Dr Diana Ivanova at Leeds University. The study identified the top 10 options for reducing our carbon footprint:

Change	CO_2 reduction in tonnes per year
Live car free	2.04
Battery electric car	1.95
One less long-haul flight per year	1.68
Renewable energy	1.6
Take public transport	0.98
Refurbishment/ renovation	0.895
Vegan diet	0.8
Heat pump	0.795
Improved cooking equipment	0.65
Renewable based heating	0.64

- Individual action has a large ripple effect. Putting solar panels on your roof means that within three years on average, 20 per cent of the houses within two miles of your house will have solar panels. Talk quietly to your friends. They will see you acting. We all want to help, to do our part, but many feel overwhelmed or simply do not know where to start. Just start. Switch to a renewable electricity supplier if you have not already. It will take 10 minutes, likely save you money and have a large impact on your carbon footprint.
- At our place of work – we have huge influence over what happens at work, particularly if we have our own businesses. Much of what is listed above is applicable at a company level. So ask what your company is doing. They have the ability not only to influence those that work for them but also their customers, creating a huge ripple effect. The current gold standard is for them to become a B Corp (Benefit Corporation) – a challenging global certification that covers not only environmental practices, but also governance and equality. Essentially seeing business as a force for good.
- At a government level – global change needs a national and international response. Theories of change state that if 3.5 per cent of the population

is engaged and protesting then that is enough to create a shift in government policy. There is already great support for this. Consider joining a group such as Extinction Rebellion which has many local groups in the UK, larger organizations such as Friends of the Earth or a smaller group that is near you. They will have information about how and what to write to your MP or other government representative, as well as who else to write to and what petitions to sign. Being an activist is open to everyone in the internet age. There is no reason not to be actively engaged and taking steps. Do not leave this to others.

Finally, think about any money you have. Move to a green bank and investments. Moving your pension can have a large impact, or request that your company invests your pension scheme in a compliant pension. More details can be found at the movement founded by Richard Curtis called Make My Money Matter (www.makemymoneymatter.co.uk).

Personal Contribution

My personal plan to contribute to my local and global community is...

Home

....

....

Work

....

....

Government

....

....

In Summary

My summary of this chapter…

1. ....

2. ....

3. ....

Key Points

1. Our relationships play a major part in determining not only how happy we are but also how long we live.

2. Prioritizing them, spending time on them, is hard as they do not make the same demands of us that work does.

3. We need to work together as individuals to prevent the human race from becoming extinct.

CHAPTER TWELVE

Work

We have looked to broaden the definition of work from a narrow view of paid employment to include what we spend our days doing. Could work be essentially the time we spend helping others? For parents much of the time spent with children can feel like work and as discussed in the previous chapter is arguably the most important work of our lives.

Work may be paid or unpaid, alone or in groups, productive or not. It is, however, a central source of identity, satisfaction, purpose and relationships. It needs to be linked back to all the hard work you did in Chapter 7 on finding your purpose (*see also* pages 71). If our work does not fit with our purpose we have no chance of a fulfilled Maverick Life. Work is likely to be the *main* expression of your purpose. We need to get it right. I include in this chapter not just your occupation, but giving, learning and productivity, all of which are crucial to the overall sense of contentment in this area of life.

Feeling like your work is meaningful is very personal. For example, there is the possibly apocryphal story of J.F. Kennedy and the cleaner. The story goes that he was touring NASA and got chatting with a cleaner. When he asked the cleaner what his role was the man replied straight away that he was helping put a man on the moon. He understood that his role was part of the bigger mission, a mission that he found both meaningful and motivating.

If you do not believe in the bigger mission, or do not believe that your role plays a part in that mission, then it may be time to move on. People find different work meaningful; you can adopt your own definition of meaning rather than just assuming it is the same as everyone else's.

Work dominates our lives and spills over into all areas. The authoritarian boss is tougher on their children at home. The stressed executive starts to notice health problems. The worker who feels like a cog in the wheel starts to become depressed and withdraws from their relationships. Can we move to a sense of part-time work for a full-time life? For some of us, part-time might still be five days a week but fewer hours in each day. For others, one or two days a week of paid work alongside other work might be the balance we need and want.

Julia Colegate-Stone was a lawyer working in finance. She could not see how her life was compatible with creating a family in the way she wanted to. She wanted to keep doing interesting and challenging work while also having the flexibility to give her children time and attention so she took a transitional role at a fast-growth company to see how she found life in a smaller business. Julia saw what an impact she could have coming from a larger, more corporate firm into a start-up. She also realized she was passionate about helping professional women find flexible work that allowed them to continue to progress their careers and be at home for the amount of time that felt right to them.

She put the two ideas together, took a deep breath and founded a firm that helped people leave blue-chip life and find part-time work that suited them. The transitional role helped Julia overcome her fears and anxieties about starting her own business. It also allowed her to discover something which she was passionate about and that the world really needed. She had found her Maverick Life.

If you are not happy with your work, you are not alone. Gallup found that, in the US, only 13 per cent of people like their work most of the time but 63 per cent are what they call 'sleep working', where they neither hate nor like their work and a further 24 per cent hate and fear their work. Given the role of technology in blurring the boundaries between work and life, we spend an increasing amount of our time 'working'. The average person sends their first email at 7.48 a.m. and logs off at 7.15 p.m. This means that being unhappy at work has a disproportionate impact on our overall happiness. We are driven by underlying stories such as, 'I have to achieve something' or 'I have to be in control'. The Maverick, on the other hand, asks different questions – where can I have the most impact, what do I enjoy doing, what are my unique strengths?

Pillar 9: Occupation

In a world of limitless possibilities, making a definitive choice about the work we do can be debilitating. The American psychologist Barry Shwartz refers to this as the Paradox of Choice. This abundance of choice, he says, can often lead to depression and feelings of loneliness. When faced with a global job market, how do we begin to decide what would be the best work for us? We put a huge amount of pressure on ourselves to land the perfect job. The good news though is that on average a job lasts four to five years so no choice has to be for ever. There are some helpful frameworks to improve our thinking on this crucial subject.

A good place to start is to think about your heroes. Who are they and what are they doing? Now ask yourself truly and honestly if you have the talent and skills to be able to do what they do. If yes, then great – proceed. If not, think about those who are *around* your heroes, those who work for and support them. This could be an excellent place for you to apply your unique skills and was what led me to coaching founders. I tried running a company and it was not a fit for my skillset. But founders are my heroes. I tried investing in those companies, but it did not feel soulful for me; I was not uniquely talented at investing. Eventually I found my right seat as a coach: a trusted *consigliere* for founders. I was able to help my heroes with a perfect match for my unique skills.

At a more detailed level, there are three components to our occupation:

- Role – what work I am going to be doing, am I going to be on my own and self-employed or part of a team? Am I part of something that is growing, shrinking, transforming? Will I be advising, investing, operating or starting?
- Sector – what does the organization do? Is the sector healthy? Is it highly specialized (medicine) or more general (retail)?
- Location – where in the world/country/city is my work based? Am I travelling locally or internationally? What is the actual work environment like?

Part of the problem is that some of these questions are hard to determine from outside a company. I had an epiphany at an immersive theatre night, where I experienced in a single night being a university lecturer, TV chef and detective inspector, among other jobs. What it made me realize (apart from how great the evening would be for people trying to decide on their career) was how much simple things like environment, colleagues and clients matter. This may sound obvious, but thinking and questioning deeply about *where* you spend your day (location), *what* you are doing and *who* you are doing it with is crucial (role and sector).

In his book, *How to Find Fulfilling Work*, Roman Krznaric has an exercise called Imaginary Lives. He asks you to imagine five parallel universes where you have a whole year off to pursue whatever career you want. Write down those five jobs and have a good think about what they entail (rock star was one of mine, as were barrister and university professor). Once you have these, how do you assess each one? What factors or criteria do you use? For many of us, money is seen as a big factor but what else? Manpower found five key priorities for millennials: money, security, time off, great people and flexible working.

It amazes me how often people describe their careers as 'Then company x approached me and then I moved to company y because they made me a great offer'. This may work for you, but at least every five years I recommend a complete review and re-appraisal of your career and job. Making a positive proactive choice to stay in your company or sector is very different to staying through inertia or a lack of curiosity.

With clients I use an exercise called the 'right work'. It focuses on teasing out what is most important to them about work (their needs or criteria) and then looks at where they are most likely to have those needs met.

These are the top five needs that people identify:

- the values and culture of the business
- interesting work
- autonomy at work
- financial reward
- great team.

Use the exercise below to list out your needs. Spend time on this. Involve others – a partner, a friend or a coach – as doing this on your own tends to trigger the same repetitive thought patterns.

The Right Work

When you have a list of the needs that are important to you for your work, write them down in the first column of the table on the next page. Now rank them in the second column in order of importance with 10 being the **most** important and 1 being the **least** important. Write the ranking in the second column.

Now add a score in the third column from 1–5 that is based on your current work. You can also add extra columns for the work or job that you are assessing. A low score of 1 would be if you do not have this aspect or need met, a high score of 5 would be if the work you are scoring meets that need well. Finally, multiply the second and third column to get the fourth column and calculate the total for the fourth column. Check that you have ranked your most important need as 10, not 1.

Important aspects	**Ranking**	**Score**	**Ranking * Score**
e.g. Empowerment	*6*	*3*	*18*
Total			

For scores of less than 130, a job move is probably the right solution for you; for 130–200, it may be a job move or changing how you work within the current environment (job crafting). Above 200? You are on your way to finding a calling and will probably stay where you are but keep working on your score.

When you have done that, you can extend it to the five jobs in your parallel universes. It can be hard to imagine how well a job might meet your criteria, do some research first. Ask people who work in that sector/company, read up on what is in the public domain, go for interviews. Gather as much information as you can for this decision and be proactive.

For many people being an entrepreneur is one of their five parallel universe jobs. It is hard to really understand what it is like to start and build your own business. I have developed a few questions here that give you some insight into how well suited you may be for this route. Write down your score from 1 being totally disagree to 5 being strongly agree.

Entrepreneur Profile

1. I am comfortable taking risks in my work life
2. **I do not need certainty about the future**
3. I am a self-starter, I do not need people to manage me
4. I am comfortable working on my own
5. I am good at dealing with stress
6. **Work-life balance is not important to me**
7. I am known as being single-minded
8. **I do not need to have friends at work**
9. I have a good network that I use regularly
10. I am aware of my strengths and weaknesses
11. I value feedback and act on that feedback
12. **I am known as a good salesman**
13. I have a track record of tangible success that is down to me alone
14. I know my approach and I tend to stick to it
15. **I can see a problem that I urgently want to solve.**

The bold questions score double so if you gave a 3 for question 2, that now counts as a 6 towards the total. Add up the total and check in with the ranges below:

1–50: time to think twice about whether starting your own business is right for you.
50–65: you are in the range – look back at some of the lower-scoring questions. Are there areas you can improve or partner with someone?
65+: at a first look you have lots of the attributes and attitudes needed to start your own business.
You might notice that making money is not included in the list. Most of the clients I work with are motivated by doing something better, solving a problem. They are aware that they might make money from this but it is not often the primary driver.

If you are looking at working in a smaller business a common conundrum is whether to lead or be a number 2. This requires some real thinking about your strengths and times in your life where you have excelled. Much as being the boss seems attractive, in many cases recognizing you are a great enabler or number 2 can be less stressful and more rewarding.

In their book *Rocket Fuel*, Gino Wickman and Mark Winters describe the two key senior roles in any business as the Visionary and the Integrator. Put simply, the Visionary is the dreamer, the seer, the creator. The Integrator is the right hand, the steady force. They argue convincingly that it takes both roles to build a great business: two entrepreneurs acting as equal partners but with very different roles. If you had a train network, think of the Visionary as the person who is deciding where to build new stations, raising the money and thinking what future trains might look like. The Integrator makes sure the trains run on time. Both roles are crucial and there is no 'better' role. Look back on the answers you gave to the questions on the previous page are you the Visionary or the Integrator?

Money

Let's have a closer look at the role that money plays in this. There is nothing that occupies the collective conscience more than money. Supposed to buy us happiness, it is a way by which some people keep score and apparently it makes the world go around.

Let's bust one myth straight away. Above a certain level, money does not make you happier. The level varies by country and researcher but seems to average at around £45,000–75,000 (approximately $65,000–95,000) of income per year. There is some more recent research indicating that how people evaluated their lives in the moment (rather than looking back) did increase beyond these levels but at a relatively small level. This study also asked the question: 'To what extent do you think money is indicative of success in life?' Those who equated money and success were less happy than others who didn't hold that view.

For some, £45–75k will seem like a lot of money and for others, very little. The truth is though that this income level allows you to have a roof over your head, food on the table and potentially build up a rainy-day fund.

End of story? If you can create a household income at the £45–75k level and happiness is your main aim, then any extra income is pointless so focus your efforts elsewhere. But it's not quite that simple. We have a complicated relationship with money that drives us in ways that can be difficult to understand. Plus, most of us just do not believe the research above. Be honest with yourself. I have been studying it for 15 years and still only believe it about 70 per cent of the time. What makes this so hard to shift?

The advertising industry, for a start. Jay Walker Smith is president of a marketing firm and says we have gone from being exposed to around 500 adverts a day in the 1970s to around 5,000 per day now. Each of those 5,000-per-day adverts is selling us something that we do not need and is unlikely to make us any happier. We are saturated with messages that claim to give us the keys to happiness but are in fact doing the direct opposite.

Second is the cult of magazines, social media and celebrity. This highly curated and edited world aims to convince us that being famous and rich makes us happy. The research into millionaires is mixed. Where they do find modest increases in happiness it is because they are spending their leisure time on active experiences such as exercising, volunteering or learning rather than passively watching Netflix. Millionaires are also twice as likely to divorce – not good news given how much we know about the importance of relationships (*see also* page 60).

Money is the main reason many of my clients and friends say they feel trapped in their work. This is the same whether they are employees or founders: 'I can't afford to leave; if I just hang on another few years, I will be all set', or 'We have an expensive life'. When I ask them how long they must hang on for, or how much their lives cost, I am invariably met with silence. Let's fill that silence with some groundbreaking thinking about achieving financial freedom, which is a key aim of the Maverick Life.

We can define financial freedom as no longer having to work for money – you have enough to last you for your life. Of course, you may want to continue working, but with the freedom to choose the amount you work, in a role that you find fulfilling and is likely of benefit to others as well as yourself. When people talk about the importance of money (remember the values exercise, *see also* page 22), they are often referring to the *freedom* that money brings.

There are only two numbers you need to calculate how far you are from financial freedom. The first is your assets – how much you have, minus any debt you owe. The second is your needs.

I met Peter Alcaraz on a Friday. It was one of those rare meetings, perhaps only once a year, where you meet someone who truly inspires you and changes the way you think. By Sunday night I had finished his excellent book, *The Wealth Game* (as a side note, some find the word 'wealth' off-putting, but here he defines it simply as having more than you need). It is his thinking and work around calculating assets and needs that is so interesting. Alcaraz recognizes that most of us do not have the time or interest to create long complicated spreadsheets and calculate where we are financially, so we don't bother. As a warning this exercise can seem alarming, particularly if you are early in your career and do not yet have many assets. You do, however, have the advantage of time.

Financial Freedom

Grab a pen and pencil and let's work this through in real time. This is a rough first pass so five minutes tops; you can refine the numbers later. Assets are straightforward – take the value of any property you own, add cash, any shares (with an estimate for private company shares), pensions and bonds. Then subtract any debt you have. This is your numerator (the one above the line).

Needs are where Alcaraz really cuts through all the crap. He has done the detail – worrying about inflation or investment performance or changes in lifestyle – and come up with a very simple but accurate enough way of calculating your needs. He suggests you take a rough estimate of your current annual cost of living (food, housing, clothes, children, holidays, etc.). This is the net amount after tax that you spend every year, but not including irregular events like house renovation or buying a car, or at this stage any education costs.

Now take a guess at the age you will die at and subtract your current age. I chose 90 so ended up with 41. Multiply your annual cost of living by the number of years you are going to live. If for example you think your cost of living is £40,000 (approximately $50,000) and you will live 40 years then the number for your cost of living needs is £1.6 million. Clearly your needs are likely to decrease over time, but the beauty of Alcaraz's calculation is the simplicity and erring on the side of prudence.

There are some other needs to be added. If you plan to educate your children privately and through university then add an amount based on where you live. If you want to include money for care when you are elderly and this is not paid for by the state, add this too. If you want to pass money on to others (children or charity), add this as a lump sum. Then for a car if you need one, add how much you will spend over the whole period on buying new cars. If you spend £10,000 every five years, then this would be £80,000 in total to add on the 40-year life example. Finally, decide the value of the equity in the house you want to live in when you pass away. The key observation here is why work harder than you have to and end up with money that is left in your bank account or your house when you die?

If you add these together with your cost-of-living needs, then you end up with your overall Needs number – your denominator. This can range hugely and may well seem out of reach, but the good news is that it is much more within your control than your Assets number.

Assets divided by Needs gives your Freedom number. Greater than 1, you are already financially free – congratulations. Less than 1, you have some work to do.

Most of us find ourselves below 1, particularly early on in our working lives, or when we have children at home. This may be sobering, but awareness is the first step towards taking control. The Maverick then makes clear plans for a path to Freedom. There are three essential accelerants towards Freedom that Alcaraz identifies – let's call them tailwinds:

1) Time – compounding is incredibly powerful. If you have £100 today and it grows by 10 per cent per year without compounding, it takes 10 years to double; with compounding, it only takes just over seven years, as you are earning 10 per cent growth on a larger number every year. Everyone has access to compounding – it just means start generating and investing a cash surplus as early as you can.
2) Choices – the biggest barrier to freedom is your cost of living. With children, energy costs and high housing costs, this can be hard to reduce. However, spending on luxuries now hugely increases the amount of time you have to keep working later in life. There are always choices in what you spend money on. The key is to generate a cash surplus and put this to work every year. Spending does not usually bring long-term happiness but it does postpone freedom.
3) Debt – used wisely and at the right amount, debt can be a huge tailwind. Used to fund assets that grow and create income, debt can help you achieve freedom years earlier. Debt on your main home, or for buying consumables, can however be a headwind as it increases your cost of living.

Consider this example to illustrate the above points. It is 1 January and you have £25,000 (approx. $30,000) in savings and each year you generate £5,000 cash surplus once you have paid for your cost of living. You have worked hard and you really want a new car. You also want to start taking nicer holidays every year. There are three potential choices here:

1) Spend – from your savings, spend £20k on a new car. Put the remaining £5k into a savings account. From your annual surplus, spend £4k per year on holidays and put the remaining £1k into a savings account. Five years later, spend another £15k on a replacement car.
2) Save to equities – from your savings, spend £5k on a car and put the balance into shares on a public market. From your surplus,

spend £1k per year on holidays and put the rest into shares. In year five, spend a further £5k on a car.

3) Save to property – from savings, spend £5k on a car and £20k on a deposit for a buy-to-let. Borrow £80k to fund the balance. From your surplus, spend £1k on holidays and £4k per year reducing the mortgage. In year five, spend a further £5k on a car.

Let's make some very simple and for-example-only assumptions that equities (including dividends) grow at 5 per cent per year net of tax and inflation and that the property (including rent) grows at 8 per cent per year net of tax and inflation. The savings account grows at the same rate as inflation after tax. Of course, things could be very different but these rates are not unheard of and are to illustrate the principle here. Let's also look over 10 years, assuming your cars are worth nothing at the end of this period. The table below shows the value of your net assets based on these different choices.

Total net assets (assets less debt)			
	Year 1	**Year 5**	**Year 10**
Option 1 – spend	£6,000	–£5,000	£0
Option 2 – save to equities	£25,000	£55,710	£93,204
Option 3 – save to property	£32,000	£81,933	£170,892

I find this table sobering. Small decisions we make now about how we spend our money have a huge impact on when, or if we ever achieve financial freedom. Left to our own devices we tend to spend what we make. The truth is that without generating and investing a cash surplus the only way you will be on the road to freedom is through acts beyond your control, such as the lottery or inheritance. I do not think this is about deprivation and living like a monk as we are unlikely to manage this. It is also never too late to start. Real pleasure can be found in both simple things in life and actually in the process of taking control and working towards your goal of financial freedom.

In their excellent book *The Art of Frugal Hedonism*, Annie Raser-Rowland and Adam Grubb explore ways to gain real pleasure and freedom from effectively managing their needs and focusing on activities that bring them joy and pleasure. I think deep down we know this to be true and that retail therapy is sometimes an inadequate replacement for psychotherapy.

Please note that I am no financial advisor and all of this is intended as a helpful guide only. Peter Alcaraz's book contains a huge amount of useful details and as always, you should seek professional advice on all aspects as you move forward on your journey in order to ensure the highest growth rates for your assets.

Working with clients, they often overestimate how much they need to achieve financial freedom. They also spend little if any time managing their own personal business and accounts as opposed to those at work.

Do you know how much you spend each month, each year and what you spend it on? Without this information you are flying blind and it is a boring but obvious place to start. It is also the first step towards taking control of your finances, of making your money work for you rather than the other way around.

Sam worked long hours in a job he did not enjoy. When I asked what kept him there, he replied that he needed another five years to get to a point where he did not have to worry about money. I asked what he meant and how he had calculated this. He gave a vague reply so I pushed him on how much he spent each year – he didn't know.

He went away and did the Financial Freedom exercise. The results surprised him. If he made some modest reductions in outgoings, he was almost at his Freedom number. He realized he had flexibility to look at other jobs that did not pay so well so he switched and was much more fulfilled.

Once you have your assets and needs calculated, the next step is to undertake a financial review. How can you reduce what you spend? For example, by switching utility companies. Making this a regular habit can help offset steeply rising costs. Challenge yourself to save at least 10 per cent of your net income. What would have to change for this to work? Many people on furlough during the COVID pandemic discovered they were able to live on 20 per cent less than usual. Some of these savings disappeared as the pandemic receded but others did not.

How about your assets, are they working for you? Are you taking up all your possible tax-free benefits in savings accounts or pensions? The earlier you start all this the better – in fact, you can set up a pension for your children and start encouraging good habits for them too.

How will you change the way you approach your work and the money you need?

1. ....

....

2. ....

....

3. ....

....

Pillar 10: Giving

For a society to function, there needs to be a self-levelling element to help keep inequality in check. Giving works for the recipient and the giver.

A 2008 study by Harvard Business School professor Michael Norton et al. found that giving money to other people lifted the participant's happiness more than spending it on themselves. That is despite participants predicting that spending it on themselves would make them happier.

There are three main ways of giving:

1) Time: whether through paid work or volunteering.
2) Money: the most obvious and talked about.
3) Network: making introductions, asking people within your network to give money or time.

Time

This is something we can all give. Once we are sure that our friends and family have enough of our time and their well-being is on track, we can turn our attention to those outside our immediate circle. There is no right or wrong amount of time to give and there will be phases in our lives (small kids, ageing parents) when we have little or no time to give outside of our homes. However, giving time is a habit. Making a commitment to a rough number of hours per week, month or year helps create and sustain that habit. Ideally, that time would be given to your community and there are good sources of finding out who needs help:

1) Local schools are always looking for governors and for people to read to children.
2) Local councils are often short of volunteers.
3) Local fêtes and events need organizing committees and volunteers.

4) Care home and elderly associations are often looking for visitors.
5) Dog owners often need dog walkers.

Decide what causes you really care about and then start researching. There are databases of volunteering opportunities such as Do-it.org in the UK.

Be wary of over-committing and always put a potential finish date on your commitments. Suggest that you will try for six months or a year and then re-evaluate. Getting stuck doing something you are not enjoying just breeds resentment on your part and in the end there will be someone better suited out there.

According to William MacAskill we spend on average 80,000 hours working over our lifetimes. MacAskill is a Scottish philosopher and ethicist and an Associate Professor at Oxford University. He is a co-founder of the 80,000 Hours organization which aims to help us consider how best to use that time. While the most obvious choice would be to work for a non-profit, often you can have as much or more impact from within a large for-profit corporate.

After 10 years of research, 80,000 Hours believe the level of impact you can have in different career paths is driven by four main factors:

1) How pressing are the problems you focus on.
2) How effective are the solutions you pursue.
3) The amount of leverage you can apply to those solutions.
4) Your personal fit for the path.

You can read more at their website www.80000hours.org

Money

When Microsoft's Bill Gates gives $100m, headlines are made. To be clear, though, that is the same as the median American giving $97.

When Gates gives $10m, that is the same as the median American giving $10. We can all give something.

Deciding how much and to whom can be difficult, which is where Effective Altruism comes in. This is a philosophy and social movement focused on answering one question: how can we best help others? The movement is also co-founded by William MacAskill. They use evidence and reason to find the most promising causes to work on. They then encourage us to act using our time and money to do the most good we can. We are often moved to give money to causes that are close by or that tug our heartstrings. This is important but may not be the most effective use of our time or money.

Their main program is the *Give What You Can* pledge, which builds up to a headline of giving 10 per cent of your income for the rest of your life. This might sound like a great deal, but during the pandemic many people realized they could live off 10–20 per cent less than they had done previously. The point is not to give so much that it impinges on your ability to lead a comfortable life, more to give the amount that allows you to balance this with helping others who are less fortunate. By finding that balance you become a beacon for others and your enthusiasm and levels of contentment become infectious.

Network

One way of expanding your impact would be to help someone else learn about and take the 10 per cent pledge. This would effectively double your giving. Imagine if you could, over your lifetime, help 10–20 others to take the pledge. That would be incredible. More broadly being an advocate in your family and clan for giving, talking about what you do gently in a show-not-tell way is immensely powerful.

The other part of Network is making introductions to those that need them who are having a positive impact. Or just directly asking people you know to give their time or meet someone who needs to pick their brains. This is much easier when you are modelling good giving.

The network effect really is not to be underestimated. Establishing your own system of giving and then talking about it among those you are close to creates a ripple effect. Remember, giving does not just help others, it helps you too.

Giving

How are you going to decide what the right level of giving is for you and put it into action?

....

....

....

....

Pillar 11: Learning

The brain is designed to learn. Learning is essential for our survival. The passing down and development of complicated knowledge from generation to generation is one of the skills that has made humans unique in the animal world. There is increasing evidence that learning new skills (e.g. piano or a language) has a much stronger impact on our brain than doing puzzles such as Sudoku or Wordle.

When we learn, we form new pathways in the brain, a process known as neuroplasticity. The benefits of neuroplasticity range from recovering from brain injury through to increased memory and cognitive abilities, as well as a virtuous circle of more effective learning.

We are programmed to seek novelty. This is how we used to discover new places to find food or ways of avoiding being eaten. Now if we do not have novelty we can wither and turn to ways of self-medicating in the forms of food, alcohol or sex. Ideally, we would find novelty in our Occupation and a lack of it can prompt the desire for a job change. In addition, looking for ways to learn outside of our occupation is essential to our enjoyment of life.

Learning is also a key component of making changes in our lives. Mavericks make planned transitions rather than impulsive leaps. Part of the reason for a timely transition is that it allows you to learn the new skills or ideas needed on your Maverick Path.

It is now possible to construct your own set of courses or talks perfectly tailored to what you need – a sort of personal life MBA. Most university courses are now available online and we have access to a wealth of ideas from leading thinkers through organizations like TED, whose slogan is 'ideas worth spreading'. Learning like this may also enable you to turn a hobby into a side or main hustle. At the very least it allows you to run experiments and see what happens. What are you drawn to learning about? What other ways of learning can you introduce to your life?

For years I let my piano playing slip. As a youngster, I played but stopped after school as I did not have anyone to encourage and stretch me. I used to drag my keyboard with me every time I moved house in the mistaken belief that this would be the time to start practising again. In the end it was finding a teacher that changed the direction of travel. It was less important who the teacher was, more that here was someone holding me accountable and making me practise.

Using time outside of work, learning things that you find fun is a great way to reap the benefits of neuroplasticity and slow cognitive decline. Instead of always running around your backhand at tennis, why not get some lessons? Always wanted to do jujitsu? Now is the time. Subject to the overall pacing of life that is discussed in your

Maverick Plan in the next chapter, it is good to have a skill you are working on learning, perhaps one at work and one outside of this.

There are many ways of learning. Reading and travelling introduce new ideas or places to your brain. Dancing is not only fun but also a way of creating new or deepening relationships.

Learning

What are you going to learn and how?

....

....

....

....

Pillar 12: Productivity

Often, we feel overwhelmed. Too much to do, not enough time in the day; emails backing up, stuck on a treadmill. Not getting to the things we really want to or need to. We tend to be ruled by the urgent things that are inbound through email or other channels, while not spending enough time identifying the important things that we need to work on. However, we need to find a way of acting as gatekeepers to the precious resources of our attention, time and energy.

One way of dealing with this is to look at what we are doing and see whether we are focusing on the right activities that fit our own definition of success. If we have too many spinning plates, then much like a computer with too many windows open, we will slow down and eventually crash.

Often it is worrying about things that we are making no progress on, paying no attention to, that clogs up our minds. Start by making a list of these open windows in the left-hand column below – tax returns can be a favourite or getting on top of emails, or there might be bigger topics such as finding a new house. Once you have done this add desired outcomes for each of them. There are a lot of rows below as once you start the list, many things tend to come out so don't be afraid to continue on a separate sheet.

Open Windows

Open window/spinning plate	**Desired outcome**

What do you notice? More than you thought? Some may not have an outcome while others may just drop off having written them down. You probably feel lighter somehow having made the list.

How many windows do you think you can tackle at any one time? Highlight and even order the ones that you want to work on. Add an action next to these highlighted windows. Now take a look through your diary for the last three weeks and the next three weeks and see how these activities fit with your new focus. What can you cancel/postpone and what do you need to add?

Check you have identified the windows you are going to focus on, the outcomes you want to achieve, and the first action you are going to take. How you keep track of the actions is up to you. Some use a paper to-do list, others prefer a digital option such as Things, Todoist or the native systems embedded in Apple or Google ecosystems. Having this list written down somewhere does help. The brain is for having ideas, not holding onto them, so generating a list allows the brain to relax and focus on creative thought rather than constantly scanning and cross-referencing a virtual 'to-do' list. This is also a moment to create a *don't-*

do list – what are you going to avoid doing, what do you get tempted into and need to resist?

I often see clients start out well having done this and gradually fall back into a state of being overwhelmed. One of the key skills they are missing is the art of saying no. Many of us find it hard to set clear boundaries – we do not want the other person to feel rejected, we worry that we might not get another opportunity, or we are just not sure if we want to do it or not. Practising saying no is a crucial Maverick skill. Clearly communicating the reason for the refusal can reduce the chances of the other person feeling hurt. The art of the graceful, or elegant, no involves explaining gently the reasons behind the refusal. Comparing the opportunity to your goals, your purpose and your definition of success can also help screen out opportunities that do not fit.

There are other options for keeping on track. In his excellent book *Getting Things Done*, Dave Allen identifies four options for dealing with action overload:

- Do – if an action takes less than two minutes, get it done there and then
- Delete – if the action does not fit with your priorities or is not moving things forward, delete it
- Defer – this can be incubated and picked up later. Make sure you have a safe place for these actions, outside of the brain
- Delegate – are you really the only person and the best person who can do this action?

What role does technology play in productivity? There has never been a more rapid take up of technology in the history of mankind than the smartphone. Wired technology such as electricity and landlines can take up to 100 years to achieve saturation. Wireless innovations such as TV and radio are quicker at around 20 years. Smartphones have been quicker still. Our moral, legal and intellectual capabilities have simply not kept up; worse still, our brains have been kidnapped.

Every day, the average American adult scrolls through a vertical band of digital materials 90m high, or the same height as the Statue of Liberty. More startling is that smartphone users in the United States consume, on average, 12 hours of media each and every day. That's more than 182 uninterrupted days of digital material, pushed through the eyes and ears of each person, every year.

Let's consider what drives this usage: news, social media, email, shopping, messaging, gaming and consuming media. Look at this list – does your heart rejoice? No, it's a list associated with increased levels of anxiety, depression and inattention. This has a serious impact on our health and our productivity. According to Microsoft our average attention span had dropped from 12 seconds in 2000 to eight seconds by 2013. Our endless and personalized content is being selected by algorithms designed to maximize the time spent consuming. Why? Because the money is made in advertising: the longer we stay on, the more advertising we consume.

Still not convinced that technology is harming our productivity? Research published by Kristen Duke in the *Harvard Business Review* in 2018 asked participants to complete cognitive tasks with their phone on their desk, in their pocket or in a different room. The results were striking: individuals who completed these tasks while their phones were in another room performed the best, followed by those who left their phones in their pockets. In last place were those whose phones were on their desks. The amazing result is that this was shown even if the phones were switched off. The impairment in cognitive ability was similar to that caused by lack of sleep.

We may think that technology has made us more productive – yes, we can consume more information, but often it is not central to our key areas of focus. It does not help us move our desired outcomes forwards.

If you are now determined to do something about this, here are six ways to permanently reduce your digital dependency:

1) **Charging station at home**. Put a box with a charger plugged in by the door that you enter your house through. As you walk through the door, the phone goes on charge in the box until you walk back out again. This has an added side benefit of losing your phone less. (If you are prone to losing your keys and wallet/purse, find a bigger box and put them in there straight away when you arrive home.)
2) **Take email and social media off your smartphone**. This is tough, but without doubt has the biggest impact. If you need these for work, fine – sit down in your office or at home with a computer or tablet and do email/social media there. Just adding that additional barrier guarantees a major reduction in time spent on your phone and indeed on these activities. Email gurus talk about working on email twice a day at 12 and 4 p.m. – not having email on your phone takes you a big step closer to achieving this liberating technique.
3) **Change your news habit**. Daily/hourly/minute by minute consumption of news is not good for us. It keeps us on high alert. Clients have found that switching to a weekly longer-form news consumption frees up huge amounts of time during the day and rapidly reduces anxiety.
4) **Phone and tablet off and put away during any conversation with a fellow human being**. Your phone, even when off, exerts a gravitational pull on your attention. Worse still, it subliminally signals to the other person that there are things going on in your life that are more important than this interaction.
5) **Black and white mode on your phone**. This is hidden way down the sub menus on an iPhone. The red notification dots are chosen deliberately – red is the colour in nature that shows danger and highjacks our ancient reptilian brain. Even a Zen Buddhist might struggle to ignore the red dot. Running your phone in black and white just makes it less appealing to spend time on.

6) **All notifications off**. If someone really needs to get hold of you, they will. Do you really need to be disturbed from your meaningful activity to know that the latest version of Angry Birds is now available? Turning off vibrate also helps with this. Better still, turn off your phone completely.

I'm not going to pretend these are easy. I lapse frequently and many of my clients are on 0, 1 or 2 out of 6. What I do know is that when I have all six of the items listed above under control, my anxiety levels are lower, I am present in a profound way and my output skyrockets.

Perhaps try one at a time. The screen time app on your phone will help you track your progress and like an ex-smoker finding themselves with bonus cash every week, you will find yourself with bonus time when you are relaxed and present to really enjoy the activity you intentionally choose.

At the start of our consultation Jim slumped down in the chair, saying he was totally overwhelmed and did not know where to start. He couldn't think clearly, was working long hours but seemed to be falling further behind; he felt low energy and everything seemed like hard work.

We started by talking about his routines outside of work. His normal routine of yoga, cycling and creating a morning or afternoon per week to think had dropped off in the last few weeks. A reset was needed and we looked through his diary for the following weeks to figure out what could be cancelled and how he could re-establish his routines. He came up with a tick box chart for his daily practices, being a visual person.

We did the open windows exercise on page 179 – the list was long. Jim agreed to focus on three key windows and to park everything else for the following three weeks. He also agreed to have a default 'no' on any new requests for his time over the following six weeks. Starting with a 'no' was a helpful shift in his thinking – he is a person who wants to say 'yes'. Finally, we reviewed his to-do list: what could be done by others and what was related to windows not in the top three priorities. This process cut the list by two-thirds.

Four weeks later, Jim was back in his exercise routines, his energy levels were up and he felt lighter, like he was making good forward progress.

Boosting your Productivity

What change are you going to make to improve your productivity?

. . . .

. . . .

. . . .

. . . .

In Summary

My summary of this chapter…

1. . . . .

2. . . . .

3. . . . .

Key Points for the Do Section

1. Work dominates our lives without us realizing it so we need to reprioritize self and others.

2. Mavericks need to create autonomy to have intentional lives. Even if we do not start our own businesses, we can live in a more entrepreneurial way.

3. We can stop at enough, it is the external motivations that keep us striving unnecessarily.

4. Often we create unnecessary stress in our lives – reducing this can have a huge impact on our effectiveness and state of mind.

5. We need to combine mental and physical approaches – the mind and body are inseparable.

6. Creating a routine that works for us around sleep, exercise and nutrition is the starting point.

7. Our relationships play a major part in determining not only how happy we are but also how long we live. Prioritizing these relationships, spending time on them is hard as they do not make the demands of us that work does.

8. We need to co-operate on a global scale in an interconnected way rather than as individuals to avoid the human race becoming extinct.

9. Work can be broadly defined as what we spend our days doing when we are not resting or relaxing. Paid or unpaid, it defines us and our impact on the world. It plays a central role in our

happiness and sense of satisfaction with life through expressing our purpose. Getting it right deserves our closest attention.

10. Continuing to learn both at work and outside of it is key to our well-being and cognitive function.
11. Magic happens when we are doing work that we believe in and are being highly productive. There are a few key useful shortcuts to high productivity.

PART IV

Deepen

CHAPTER THIRTEEN

Your Maverick Plan

Now it's time to pull everything we have discussed together and create your Maverick Plan. Well done for reading this far. You have covered a huge range of topics and ideas. The work we engage in now will take time but is the most important part of the book. Start by reading back through your notebook or wherever you have completed the exercises and taken notes. Remind yourself of the process you have undertaken:

- to understand what a Maverick Life looks like
- to honestly examine what matters to you and how you are doing in your life
- to think about your own personal definition of success
- to let go of the expectations of others and of yourself
- to identify your strengths and superpower
- how you apply that superpower to work with your purpose and increase your meaning in life
- to start balancing work with looking after yourself and others
- to identify pillars on your Life Quotient (LQ) score that need work and think about how to become Life Fit.

You have written down lots of ideas, resolutions and almost certainly questions too. This is when you prioritize these and set some clear targets. Please do not skip this part of the book, however tempting it is. If this feels overwhelming, that is OK and normal. This final section of the book – Deepen – helps build your motivation and creates a real momentum for change. For now, your job is to create the plan that puts you in the stretch zone, not the comfort or panic zones.

To help us do this, we're going to look at someone from the world of sport. Jurgen Grobler coached the British heavyweight men's rowing team to gold medals at every Olympics from when he came to the UK in 1991 to Rio in 2016. A period covering seven Olympic Games up to his retirement after Rio and spanning 27 years. Before that, he coached East Germany to bronze in 1972 and then gold medals in the following four Olympics in which they participated (they boycotted 1984 due to tensions between the US and the USSR). Gold medals at 11 Olympic Games spanning 40 years is an unparalleled record as a coach. At Tokyo, the first Olympics after Grobler retired, the team failed to win a gold medal.

What can we take from this extraordinary track record into our daily lives? There are three lessons that we can learn from Grobler in designing our own Maverick Plan:

1) Setting goals and having a plan
2) Measuring where you are against the plan
3) Reviewing your performance and adjusting accordingly.

Setting Goals and Having a Plan

With UK sport, Grobler would agree the next Olympic medal target for the team immediately following the Olympics. There was always at least one gold medal in the target, so to reach this goal, he would predict the time the top crew would need to row four years later to win gold. That gold medal time became the basis for the four-year plan. There is nothing clearer or simpler than creating the goal of rowing the race on Olympic final day in the Gold medal winning time, the trick was deciding the time four years before the final. Time for you to figure out what race you want to enter and what time you need to win it.

Without setting goals you will lack focus and direction. Your Maverick Path will be stop-start or may even fizzle out altogether. This is key to taking control of your life's direction, to building autonomy and freedom. Set goals that motivate you, meaning that they are important to you and your purpose, and relate to your priorities in life that have emerged as you have been reading this book. It is key to write these goals down, as stated earlier, having them in your head does not count and is ineffective.

Clients often ask me what time frame to set goals for, how to set them and what areas they should cover. Start with a wish-list set of ideas and dreams for 10 or even 20 years based on your definition of success, however crazy they seem. How would you like your life to look in 20 years' time? Where are you living, who are you with, what are you doing? Now go back to your 80th-birthday exercise (*see also* page 84), remember where you were in 20 years' time? These are high-level aspirations.

I once worked with a client who had their own business co-located with where they lived. It was a family business that they had grown dramatically since taking over 17 years ago. We spent most of our time together thinking about the now or the next 12 months but when we began to talk about a 20-year timeline the whole conversation changed. They realized that they wanted to be not only out of the business in 20 years' time, but also living in a different place to give their children a chance to breathe and develop the business in their own way. This vision created some shorter-term actions such as starting to talk to their children and spending time away from the business. It also created a framework to develop some detailed mid-term goals.

The next step is to think about a broad five-year vision. Keep it reasonably high-level at this stage. Perhaps financial freedom is in there, maybe a change of location. Think about what age you will be in five years' time, what age your children will be (if you have them or are thinking of having them). Discuss this with friends, your partner, your family or your coach.

Now work your way towards some more detailed three-year goals and then specific one-year goals. The shorter the time frame, the more specific you can be. Setting three to seven goals gives the best chance of success. You can look back to your Life Quotient (LQ) score (*see also* pages 35–40) to see which pillars might benefit from having a goal ascribed to them.

Now check your goals using the slightly formulaic but very effective SMART framework:

- **S**pecific – is the goal clear, who needs to be involved, what sort of actions are needed?
- **M**easurable – how will you know when you get there? What are the key indicators that you need to put in place and measure?
- **A**chievable – can you accomplish this goal? Do you have the resources and levels of control that you need to do this?
- **R**elevant – consider your big picture goals, the longer-term vision. Does this goal fit into the overall framework? Is this the right time to be setting this goal? Does it fit with your purpose and your values? If there is a conflict here, the goal is likely to fail.
- **T**ime-bound – when does this need to be completed? What steps do you need to take in the coming weeks and months? What are the key milestones that let you know you are on track?

Imagine a goal of financial freedom. How would you make that a SMART goal? For example, something like 'I will be financially free (assets greater than needs) by 31 December 2030'.

If you panic when reading your goal then it may not be achievable. You may need to push the date out or choose a smaller interim goal. If you do not find it motivating, it's probably not relevant – check that it still aligns with your purpose and values.

Pacing

We all try to do too much in too short a time span. Not only do we underestimate how long things take to do properly, we try to manage too much in parallel. Remember the open windows exercise in the previous chapter (*see also* page 179)? The work I do with the senior team of one client is deeply rewarding. Each year we retreat for two days to plan the following year and each year they leave the retreat with *less* on their list than when they arrived. They increase their focus, slow their pace and figure out how to increase quality as they grow at the right pace for them. Think about your pace, knowing this is a long-term plan: what is the right pace for you that you can sustain? If we try and sprint a marathon, we end up in hospital (unless we are Eliud Kipchoge, who covers a marathon at the equivalent pace of 16 seconds per 100m).

The second point about pace is that our plan cannot anticipate exceptional items. For example, we may have to care for an elderly relative or a colleague might be long-term sick. We ourselves may become injured or be asked to work on a time-sensitive project that we simply cannot refuse, so allow slack in the system. If we start with our days, weeks and months full then we are bound to fail. I urge clients to leave at least a day per week unplanned to pick up exceptional items and if there is still space to use it for thinking time. OK, it's hard to do this but essential for a long-term plan.

As well as pace, we all need to think about timings and approach to transitions. Much like a DJ, we need to fade in new tracks and fade out old ones. Occasionally I see clients who have just had enough and want to quit on the spot. If they really do need to quit then they are six to 12 months past the point where it would have been ideal to start thinking about a transition plan. Mostly we work on creating that six- to 12-month plan – just having a plan makes their day more tolerable. During the period you can start a side hustle, you can do courses if you need to add skills or knowledge to your repertoire; you can even plan an orderly exit from your current workplace. We all have more power than we realize and often others around us will be up for enabling a transition rather than just being thrown back the keys.

Your Maverick Plan

We all have different ways of representing a plan. If you have your own way, please use it. The plan needs to live and breathe, not get stuck in a notebook, on a hard drive or in a drawer so put it on the wall, show it off, live with it. If you prefer digital, that's fine – just find a way to check in with it regularly.

The best example I have seen came from a client called Charlie Bradshaw. He used to pull out his laminated A4 version in our sessions, flourishing it like a master map. I have included the outline of it below to give you a template to help construct your own Maverick Plan.

Start by adding your Purpose Statement that you created in the exercise on page 81. This provides a frame of reference for your plan. Does it need tweaking? How is it sitting with you?

Now go ahead and add your three- and five-year goals as a useful reminder and reference point. Next look at your goals covering the next year and pick the things that are most important for you to be working on. They must be goals that you cannot delegate, likely a mix of work and non-work. Often clients have one goal based around health or learning, as we saw from the previous chapter (**see *also*** page 178). There are five columns below, which is a maximum – it is sometimes better to have three to four goals to focus on as we lose efficiency as we increase the number of plates we are trying to keep spinning.

Use the next row to define what success looks like at the year end or in 12 months' time. Then crucially write down the people you need to brief and involve in the next row. Finally, in the third row are the critical actions for the next three months. You can then transfer the first action in each of these columns over to your to-do list. Review this weekly and quarterly, updating the actions as needed.

These goals are hard to achieve, particularly on your own. Research from the Association for Talent Development finds the following odds on an individual achieving a particular goal:

- ten per cent if all you have is an idea;
- twenty-five per cent if you decide to take action on this goal;
- forty per cent if you have a deadline;
- fifty per cent if you have a step-by-step plan for how to meet your goals;
- sixty-five per cent if you commit to someone that you will meet your goals;
- ninety-five per cent if you have a specific meeting with someone to whom you have made yourself accountable.

There are ways of holding yourself to account. SMART goals help with clear actions and deadlines, but you can double your chances of success by involving someone else but who to pick as your accountability partner? If you work in a company, you probably already have one for work – your boss – but the point of a Maverick Life is that you are your own boss, so how do you recreate that sense of accountability? Select someone who is strong enough to give you honest feedback, even if it hurts your feelings or is upsetting to you. Friends and family can help here but it is preferable to have someone who can be more objective. Perhaps they are also working on goals so you can hold each other to account?

This highlights the power of coaching. One of the underpinnings of the practice is that your coach acts as your accountability partner. They are completely objective and ready to call you out on any blind spots or just general self-delusion. Once you have your plan, the last piece of the puzzle is finding a way of being accountable. The key is not only picking your partner but fixing up a regular check-in with them, maybe weekly or monthly at the beginning of your Maverick journey. Could you also act in return to keep them accountable for changes they are looking to make?

Purpose Statement and Goals

My Purpose Statement is…

....

....

Five-year Goals

1. ....

2. ....

3. ....

Three-year Goals

1. ....

2. ....

3. ....

I am accountable to…

....

....

I will meet with them every…

....

....

	Goal 1	Goal 2	Goal 3	Goal 4	Goal 5
What does success look like for me on 31 December 20__ (or in 12 months)?					
Next quarter critical actions					
Key relationships to deliver this success					

Measuring Where You Are Against the Plan

Let's return to the example from our Olympic coach, Jurgen Grobler. In the summer months when the crew was honing its racing speed, there would occasionally be flat-out timed efforts over the race distance. This would then give a percentage of the gold medal time, where the aim was to be at 100 per cent on finals day. The progress towards this goal was a crucial indicator of how well the plan was going.

There is a saying in business that you manage what you measure. Really what this means is that we influence and change what we choose to focus on. Companies spend a lot of time figuring out what their Key Performance Indicators (KPIs) are and then reporting against them. What would your personal KPIs be? These are measures that you can look at to help you gauge where you are against your own personal plan, your own definition of success. They might include health measures, financial measures, impact measures, family time measures, giving back measures – any number of possible areas that you choose to focus on. This unique personal 'dashboard' would ideally tie into your goals and provide a regular opportunity to assess where you are against your plan.

Now return to your Maverick plan in the exercise above. Check the success at year-end row. Are there KPIs in here? For example, if health is a focus area, could there be a KPI around weight, resting heart rate or sleep? If learning is a key focus, how could you measure progress in this area? When I was putting my piano playing back on track, a KPI was to perform one of Chopin's Nocturnes to my family at the year end. It was a terrifying goal but kept me on track and practising.

Reviewing Your Performance

While KPIs might be useful for understanding whether or not you are on track, they do not always shine a light on what you could be doing differently. In his book, *Will it Make the Boat Go Faster?*, Ben Hunt-Davis argues for a daily reflection of performance. Hunt-Davis won gold in the 2000 men's rowing eight at the Sydney Olympics, having come sixth and eighth in the previous two Olympics. The team turned their prospects around by asking the same question after every outing: how did we perform today and what can we do to make the boat go faster? He argues that by focusing on performance then the results will take care of themselves. A proper performance review requires as he describes it 'proper bullshit filters'. In a team environment it takes great honesty and mutual respect, alongside an agreed set of behaviours.

From a different perspective the Dalai Lama, in his work *The Book of Joy*, talks about a morning and evening routine that ensures the best from the day. The morning starts with some deep breaths and then focusing on what your heart's desire is before turning this into an intention for the day. The evening reflection is reviewing that intention, feeling gratitude and rejoicing in a highlight. What a lovely performance review.

You can begin to see the power of a regular meeting with an accountability partner here: it forces you to take the performance review seriously and prepare for it. What do you do with the output of a performance review? Well, you need to course correct. Much like the fact that 93 per cent of successful businesses do not make it on their original idea, so your first Maverick Plan is unlikely to be the perfect one. No fudging here, just an honest look at how you are doing and an acceptance that there will be setbacks. No setbacks means you are most likely deluding yourself and that consigns you to a non-Maverick Life.

Check the focus areas match your purpose and priorities. Make sure you have the right people involved. Check your actions are directly linked to making progress. If you do not already have a coach in your life, this is an excellent time to find one. Ask around, or visit www.themodernmaverick.com for more details. Your workplace may also have a list of approved coaches.

In Summary

My summary of this chapter…

1. ....

2. ....

3. ....

Key Points

1. The brain needs a clear plan and a set of goals to create forward momentum.
2. Finding and meeting with an accountability partner is essential in making the plan a reality.
3. Using KPIs to make an honest assessment and course correction is a normal and critical part of executing a successful plan.

CHAPTER FOURTEEN

Making Effective Changes

Many of us, particularly if you are reading this book, will have contemplated change before. There will have been times when you have successfully made changes and other more frustrating times when either the change has not happened or there has been a retreat to the old way.

There has been a great deal of research on change and the various stages. One of the best-known models was developed by James Prochaska and Carlo DiClemente in the early 1980s, based on a study of people trying to quit smoking. They found six key stages:

1) **Pre-contemplation.** In this stage there is denial of the problem. Moving out of this stage involves asking yourself some questions, such as have you tried to change before, what would have to happen for you to consider your behaviour a problem, what would others close to you say?
2) **Contemplation.** The benefits of making a change start to become clearer, as do the costs. Asking why you want to change, what is preventing you from changing and what could help you make this change can be helpful.
3) **Preparation.** Experimenting with small changes and writing motivating statements is helpful at this stage. Also recruiting others such as a coach, friend or support group, who can help keep you on track.

4) **Action.** This is when you are taking clear and direct action towards a goal. Rewarding success is key to maintaining progress, as is reviewing motivation and pulling in other resources to help.
5) **Maintenance.** Sometimes the hardest stage. Look for ways to avoid temptation and if you do slip up, be kind to yourself. This is never a binary all-or-nothing process.
6) **Relapse.** Common in any behavioural change, relapses bring about feelings of disappointment and failure. The key here is to accept this happens, understand what triggered the relapse and then start again with preparation, action or the maintenance stage.

Which stage do you think you are in? You can be at different stages for different goals. Change is hard. We become attached to the familiar, it keeps us safe. As we move beyond our comfort zones into the stretch zone, our inner voices chime in, 'You will fail, it will be stressful, go back to what you know.' Our stories and limiting beliefs kick in. If we try to take on too much change too quickly, we jump into our panic zones and our parasympathetic systems from Chapter 10 (*see also* page 113) kick in to keep us hyperalert. It is so uncomfortable in the panic zone that any prolonged exposure here pushes us back into our comfort zones, change abandoned.

Remember the six forces in Chapter 6 (*see also* pages 54–7)? These keep us tethered in place, reassuring us that we are on the right track, that externally we are making effort in the right places. These forces are an almost constant presence in our lives, they create resistance to change. It is worth going back and looking at your answers to the exercise on page 56.

We also set ourselves up to fail by setting high or even perfect expectations. Perfectionism keeps many people in an uncomfortable part of their comfort zone. Knowing they need to change, they procrastinate until the last minute. At that point they either abandon change altogether as there is just not enough time to get the job done at all or make a poor effort, consoling themselves that it is not their fault – they just did not have enough time.

Perfectionism

Here are some questions to think about if perfectionism might be a problem for you:

1. Do you have standards that are too high, that you never quite reach?
2. Are you able to flex these standards when required?
3. Are these high standards always helpful to you?
4. Do you impose these standards on others and what happens when they do not meet these standards?
5. Who says you always must meet these standards?

If you have answered 'yes' to some of these questions, you are not alone. Awareness is the first step and starting to look at the costs and benefits of this behaviour. Think of a time when you last procrastinated. What was the moment where these thoughts kicked in? What were the thoughts exactly? What are the causes of these thoughts?

The key question to explore is what the benefits of these thoughts are and what are the unhelpful consequences, so make a column of each. What do you notice?

Perfectionism is also closely linked to the feeling of imposter syndrome – where you feel you do not belong somewhere, are not good enough to be there. By applying unrealistically high expectations and standards to those around you, by definition you do not belong there. If you tie your sense of self-worth to your performance, this makes receiving feedback and making improvements harder. It can also lead to not really applying yourself for fear of failure but failure is such an important part of making progress, of becoming a Maverick. Tom Watson was the CEO of IBM during its transformational growth between 1956 and 1971. He said, 'If you want to increase your success rate, double your failure rate.'

Perfectionism is also one of the main reasons for procrastination. This is different from the decision to defer something that we looked at in Pillar 12: Productivity in Chapter 12 (*see also* page 181). Procrastination can be avoidance, a way of achieving control, trying to get others to do the job, having too much to do or a mistaken belief that a last-minute frenzy is the best way to get something done.

Reducing Procrastination

To deal with procrastination, go back to the moment when thoughts arise such as, 'I just do not know where to start'. Make a list of these thoughts. Next to each one write an alternative thought that is likely to help you make a start – for example, a counter to 'I don't know where to start' could be 'I will write the first paragraph'.

The second part of the exercise is to develop your own anti-procrastination coach so make a list of the first steps you can take to get going. Now add to the list ways you can maintain this progress. Perhaps you can give yourself some rewards or make yourself accountable to someone else? Finally, make a list of how getting this done is going to make you feel.

What are the clear benefits of breaking the procrastination cycle? At some point there is no substitute for *just starting*.

> 'Start by doing what is necessary, then do what is possible and suddenly you are doing the impossible.' *Francis of Assisi*

Habits are another powerful way in which we stay stuck and trapped in our current place. They emerge without our permission, are stored in an ancient part of the brain called the basal ganglia and cannot be deleted, but they can be modified.

Charles Duhigg wrote an excellent book, *The Power of Habit*, which explained the habit loop. First, there is a cue which prompts the brain to go into automatic mode. Then comes the routine, which is the physical, mental or emotional behaviour associated with the cue. Finally, there is the reward, which is the reason for the behaviour and helps the brain figure out if the routine is worth remembering.

A simple example would be snacking:

- Cue – I am bored or I am hungry
- Behaviour – leave the desk to go and find a snack, or stop working and open the desk drawer
- Reward – relief of boredom, relief of the feeling of hunger.

If you try to ignore the cue, this creates a craving that does not go away unless you have extreme willpower. Duhigg argues that the secret is to recognize the cue, keep the reward the same but change the routine so in the example above, if the cue is boredom then look for another way to relieve boredom (reward). Could you build in regular breaks? Could you go for a walk? Could you go and chat to a colleague? If the cue is hunger, could you get the same reward (not hungry) through drinking some water, having a healthy snack or waiting until your next meal?

I have a bad end-of-day habit: I arrive home after a day's work (the home office is only a 50-metre commute) and immediately reach for a snack and a beer. It feels like a reward for a day completed and signals the transition into evening time. Using Duhigg's model the cue is at the end of the day I want to unwind. The behaviour is to eat and drink, the reward is a feeling of relaxation and celebration.

The first step was to recognize the pattern. The next was to figure out alternative behaviours. For example, I could switch to an alcohol-free beer and a healthy snack, or I could seek out alternative ways of unwinding (take a bath, take some exercise) and wait for dinner to start eating. Most of the time this works, but during stressful periods like all of us I revert to the original behaviour. I am acutely conscious of doing this – one day is fine, two days and it starts to become a routine but three days and bang, the habit is back. The odd break is fine, but if it starts to stick then remind yourself of the switch you made last time that stuck.

A key part of behavioural change is the knowledge and belief that it is possible. This is where the group setting in Alcoholics Anonymous is so powerful. First, the group replaces one of the common cues for drinking, which is loneliness. Second, people see first-hand other group members changing their behaviour.

Prochaska and DiClemente who did the work on change at the start of the chapter also identified certain keystone habits that if put in place seemed to act as a gateway to other good habits. Exercise is an example. Another is eating together as a family if you do live under the same roof, which seems to help raise children with better homework skills, higher grades, greater emotional control and more confidence. Making your bed in the morning is correlated with better productivity, a greater sense of well-being and stronger skills at sticking with a budget. Keeping a food journal can double weight loss. This is not claiming cause and effect, more that an initial shift creates a chain reaction that can help other good habits take hold.

Willpower, the ability to resist short-term temptation in order to meet long-term goals, clearly has a role to play. The good news is that it is a muscle not a skill and can be trained. Psychologist Mark Muraven with colleague Roy Baumeister found that willpower gets used up. They found after participants had been forced to exert willpower vs a control group they then gave up much more easily on a subsequent cognitive task. Resisting temptation takes a mental toll. This explains why we find it harder to resist things when we are tired at the end of the day. It also shows us how to train our willpower. So, start small and build up.

Our belief in our willpower has a major impact on our actual willpower so show yourself that you can do this, pick something and gradually increase it. Running is a good example – a 10 per cent increase in distance or time every two to three weeks would be brilliant and is physiologically doable. You can develop your own reward system (commensurate with the achievement). The brain is wired for instant gratification so take advantage of this and when you have shown willpower, find a way to congratulate yourself.

This has major implications for the pace and breadth of change you are trying to make. The complete overhaul approach does not work. Focusing on one goal at a time, in series and not parallel, is a much more effective method.

You are not alone in this Maverick endeavour. Return to Chapter 3, to your constellation (*see also* page 27) and pick out three to four people who can help you make your Maverick changes. Who are those people? Talk to them, let them know what you are embarking on and that you will need help, encouragement and to be held accountable. Be clear on what you are going to do by when. Ask them to check in with you. Make sure they are people who give you energy rather than suck energy like a sponge.

Another way of ensuring we make effective changes is to build up our resilience. Like willpower, this is a muscle that grows with use – it's not something you have or don't have. The exercise below helps you measure and develop your resilience.

Resilience

Add up your resilience score using the chart below by scoring each of the building blocks of resilience depending on whether they are in great shape, OK or in poor shape. There is no positive score for alcohol/drugs for obvious reasons. Check back to your Life Quotient (LQ) if you need help (*see also* pages 35–40).

	Great	OK	Poor
Exercise	+3	+1	-2
Relaxation	+3	+1	-2
Sleep	+3	+1	-2
Diet	+2	+1	-2
Alcohol/Drugs		-1	-3
Relationships/Social	+4	+2	-3
Thought Patterns	+3	+1	-3
Emotional Control	+2	+1	-2
Me Time	+2	+1	-2

You are looking for a score of 10+, with an ideal score in the high teens. A negative score means you need to take some urgent action and is maybe a sign that you are on your way to burnout. If you have a very low score, it is worth consulting a medical professional or someone who specializes in working with cases of burnout.

Pick your lowest scores and return to the relevant sections in Chapters 10–12 (from page 105) to develop some key actions. Make sure these are included in your Maverick Plan.

Time for action. Revisit your Maverick Plan that you made in the previous chapter (*see also* pages 198–201) and identify where to start. Pick one area that is high impact on your plan and not too hard to achieve. This is a quick win – a sure-fire way to build momentum for your plan is to have some quick wins early on.

Pick the first action in that area. Now you have your action, you have your team check in with a 1–10 score on the Readiness, Importance, Confidence test:

How ready are you?

How important is this to you?

How confident do you feel?

If you score less than 8 on any of the three questions, then you need to go back and re-examine. Have you picked the right action? How do you boost your confidence, or do you start with an easier action? How do you get ready?

Let's visualize what it might feel like. Try the miracle question developed by Steve de Shazer the psychotherapist and pioneer of solution focused brief therapy: 'Imagine in six months' time we meet up coincidentally in the street. You say that the problems we are discussing today are getting better. What would you tell me had happened?'

How does it feel to imagine that? If the goal is a good one it will feel great to have crossed it off your list. Imagine telling people you have done it, think about the boost to your willpower and self-esteem.

Once you have ticked off your first win, congratulations, it's time to celebrate. We tend to just move on to the next challenge and then wonder why we run out of steam. Building momentum is about celebrating your successes as well as examining your failures. What is a reward for you? What really motivates you? Me, I am off to enjoy some sourdough toast with homemade marmalade, having finished this chapter. For me, food is a major motivator. I do have to watch that this does not become a form of self-medication though, ensuring that my weight stays within a range.

In Summary

My summary of this chapter…

1. ………………………………………………………

2. ………………………………………………………

3. ………………………………………………………

Key Points

1. Change is hard, but understanding the key stages of change and the power of habits can help progress.

2. We need to build up our key change muscles of resilience and willpower.

3. Focusing on and completing a key action is the best way to get started on your Maverick Path.

CHAPTER FIFTEEN

Staying Out of Your Own Way

At this point in the book, the challenges to the Maverick Life might seem vast. We may look enviously at others who appear to sail along unimpeded and wonder how they do it. They seem to have figured out how to be highly effective and focused. They are living a life on purpose, intentional and clearly planned. It is possible. By now you will have an increasingly clear sense of purpose, some helpful ideas and tools to hand, and an idea of how to make these changes.

This chapter looks at how we impede ourselves, how adept we can be at self-sabotage. Without realizing it, our thoughts about ourselves or what we are facing have a monumental impact on how we navigate life.

The architect Tiziano Terzani built on an idea from Epictetus the Stoic Philosopher: 'Very few people understand that what is important is not what happens but how we interpret it. The world is whatever we construct of it and we are always capable of changing our constructions.'

Often we spend time thinking about or worrying about problems that either do not exist, or that we have no control over. I call this 'shadow boxing'. It is a colossal distraction and use of resources that are much needed elsewhere.

Sarah was overwhelmed. She ran a fast-growing company and had an ever-increasing to-do list. She spent a great deal of time imagining and worrying about scenarios that were extremely unlikely to happen. This left her underprepared when some of the more real curve balls did arrive. We talked about the concept of shadow boxing, applying time and energy to amorphous problems that are not central or even likely.

She was able to identify several areas where she was doing this and to start to let go of them or focus on them if they were real and important.

Shadow Boxing

Write down two or three areas where you shadow box:

1. ....

2. ....

3. ....

How does this shadow boxing help you? What are your thoughts based on? What would an independent witness say if you laid these thoughts out? Are any of them real and important – if so, what are the actions? Do they need to go onto your Maverick Plan or can you let go of them? We cannot control everything; in fact, we can control very little. Be very careful and conscious about where you put your energy and focus.

Many of us have experienced periods, long or short, of low self-esteem. Defined as holding a psychological mirror up, self-esteem is literally our judgement of ourselves. Almost purely based on our perception of how the world sees us, low self-esteem can be a major impediment to change and a cause of ongoing anxiety or sadness. It can interfere with loving relationships and in extreme cases can lead to arrogance or self-obsession as we try to protect ourselves by projecting a sense of superiority or false confidence. In short, it underpins many psychological problems and is no fun to live with.

Look back on your lifeline that you drew in Chapter 2 (*see also* page 17). Remember how you felt when the line was going up and how differently when the line was going down. Which came first, the events or the feelings about the events? The truth is it does not matter: we can work on our self-esteem.

In Part III: Do of this book, we looked at self and separately at our relationships with others (*see also* pages 105 and 131). Self-esteem is essentially our relationship with ourself. A good relationship, where we recognize our frailties and treat ourselves with kindness, frees us up to explore our talents, make our mistakes and move on. I often see clients who treat themselves much more harshly than others. Why do they do this? No one is telling them to do so. It is very debilitating and keeps us caged in a world of self-doubt and antipathy.

Remember the fifth regret of the dying that terminal care nurse Bronnie Ware noted: 'I wish I had allowed myself to be happier.'

Permission to be Happy

Write down the answer to the question what, and/or who, is preventing you from allowing yourself to be happier?

....

....

....

....

....

So then, is the solution just to boost self-esteem? This is part of the solution but not the whole and here there is a wrinkle. Research shows that high self-esteem is the result of working hard to get good grades in school, not the cause of the good grades (Baumeister & Tierney, 2012). So here we have a classic chicken and egg conundrum. Low self-esteem makes us less likely to try, which makes results worse and reinforces the low self-esteem.

The key to unlocking this is moving from conditional self-esteem to unconditional *self-acceptance*. Unlike self-esteem, self-acceptance is based around not judging yourself but instead, looking at your actions and figuring out how to change those actions for a better result, while recognizing that we are all fragile and fallible. Self-acceptance knows that we will make mistakes – in fact, failures and upsets are the only way to evolve.

This also means focusing on accomplishment for the sake of it rather than as a way to boost your ego. It's like the difference between playing piano alone for your own pleasure rather than needing an audience to validate your performance. Instead of putting ourselves down constantly, we shift focus to curiously looking at actions, traits and experiences. When you meet someone who behaves in a way that you think is offensive, change the question from 'What is wrong with you?' to 'What happened to you?' Now try turning that question on yourself: 'What is wrong with me?' becomes 'What happened to me and how can I start to understand and accept that?'

Instead of seeing failing an exam as making you a total failure, self-acceptance is to study the actions leading up to the failure (for example, I didn't prepare enough, I misread some of the questions, I rushed my answers) and look to improve on those next time. Or you might recognize that exam conditions are not where you are at your best, perhaps due to too much pressure being applied as a child. You may hit a useless shot in tennis, but it does not make you useless, just as a wonderful shot does not make you former world No. 1 Roger Federer so cut yourself some slack – you certainly don't need to give up tennis just because you hit a bad shot.

We can also practise what psychologist Carol Dweck refers to as a growth mindset. She distinguishes this from a fixed mindset – where we believe that our intelligence, character and creativity are inherent and that any success or failure is a result of that. A growth mindset sees challenges and failures as signposts to where we can learn and grow.

Ned was a co-founder in a firm where he felt undervalued and underappreciated. When his co-founder did not include him or made a comment that seemed to belittle him, the belief that he was not valued kicked in, making him believe that he was not good enough and impacting his performance as his self-esteem dropped.

We discussed this belief that was triggered that he was not valued and looked for real evidence that this was the case. He had some direct conversations with his co-founder to try and understand some of his behaviour. It turned out that there was one area where the co-founder did feel Ned was underperforming, but in all other areas he highly valued him. Ned decided to allow his co-founder to take charge of the underperforming area and to double down on the areas where he was valued. He was able to see that he was an important part of the team and to stop looking for reasons to believe otherwise.

Comparison

'Comparison is the thief of joy' is a saying attributed to President Franklin D. Roosevelt among others. He had no idea that 100 years later it was going to be a whole lot harder not to compare ourselves to others. Today we can compare ourselves to pretty much anyone on the planet through social media and the internet. These potentially infinite comparisons are based on sketchy curated data at best and at worst, downright lies or falsifications. We compare the honest and harsh views of ourselves with the false perceptions of others. We are never going to measure up. No wonder that comparison to others, recently turbocharged by social media, is a precursor of depression. We all know it is not a good habit, but how do we stop it or even better, how do we turn it into a positive for ourselves?

One of the privileges of working as a coach is that you are privy to the insides of people, the insides of their heads and emotions, not just what they project to the outside world. In fact, much of our work is trying to close the gap between the reality and the projection – a journey to authenticity. How much do you know about the insides of others, even your closest friends and families? When you really see the inside, you realize that we are all equal in our struggle towards a calm state of mind.

Another pitfall of comparison is focusing on others and ignoring what makes you unique – what you have going for yourself. I call this the 'Bagel Effect'. In other words, we tend to look at the hole in the middle, what is missing, rather than the bagel itself. We take inflated views of the talents of others and compare them to our weak spots that we are only too painfully aware of. How about focusing on what we have, rather than what we think others might have? We have no idea how they set their priorities or where they are in their journeys. As the sportsman and author Tim Hiller said, 'Don't compare your beginning to someone else's middle, or your middle to someone else's end.'

Have you noticed that your tendency to compare, and the negative impact of those comparisons, tends to fluctuate with time? If we are experiencing low self-esteem or low confidence we tend to compare more, setting up a vicious cycle. This tends to be in times when we have lost sight of who we really are, who we are trying to be. Becoming aware of this can be a useful trigger. Instead of allowing our thought processes to loop downwards, how about taking this as a cue to make some changes?

Comparisons used in the right way can be inspiring. First, when we find ourselves comparing, let's look inside ourselves and recognize that we may be off track. Second, let's check those comparisons: are they fair, are they accurate, is the data good? Third, make sure we are marking ourselves fairly, recognizing the good in us, the uniqueness. Then and only then can we look at how we turn the remaining comparisons into inspiration rather than gloom. Perhaps the other person's journey, outlook on life or priorities are appealing to us. We can use jealousy as a signpost to where we need to make changes. When we meet someone who is calm, and calm is a desired state for us, it is natural to be curious and to ask them about it. The crucial point here is that we are with them, talking and learning, not just observing through a tweet or a photo.

This happened to me recently. I was sitting with a friend who I admire, who has a calm state of being and embraces a Buddhist approach to life. We were talking about the skewed definition of success that society ensnares us with. I asked him how he dealt with this and what his definition was. His answer was very human and honest, that sometimes he struggled with it, but in his best moments he recognized that his ability to be present and helpful to his friends, family and community was the secret.

Here was something tangible I could work with, to celebrate some of the 'non-core work' that I was doing. My comparison to him, my desire to be more like him, had yielded via a good conversation – a nugget of wisdom that I could start trying to include in my self-reckoning. So when you find yourself comparing, take note, compare well and truthfully, then look at what *you* can do.

Revisit the exercise on comparison in Chapter 5 (Comparison Points, *see also* page 50) and refine it. Keep it close on your Maverick Path as this is one of the most common pitfalls. What are other headwinds that can slow your progress?

The psychologist Raj Persaud, in his 2005 book *The Motivated Mind*, identified three other areas that can slow or prevent progress.

1) **Resource depletion.** If you are tired, long-term tired or unwell, then however clear your plan is, execution becomes twice as hard. Clear thinking becomes three times as hard. If you are struggling, go back and check the basics. Revisit the Self section in Chapter 10 and check in with Pillars 2, 3 and 4 (*see also* pages 116–29). Filling up your batteries and resource tank can take a while – days, weeks or months if you have had long-term depletion. You will know though when your tank is full enough: the world seems like a happier, easier place.
2) **Goal conflict.** It may be that the goals you have set as part of your Maverick Path conflict with your values or that you have slightly misidentified your values. Go back to Chapter 3 and re-do your values exercise (see also page 22). Sometimes you have to set short-term goals that may be in conflict or not spot on with your values. In this case, double-check your reasons for the goal and then it's a case of head down and grind it out to get it done.
3) **Inadequate tracking.** You are full of beans, your goals are spot on, but still you are not making progress. It may be that you do not have your goals at the forefront of your mind, that you are not checking in with them, allocating time to them. All this can be picked up by tracking your progress. Was the original timeline too tight or not tight enough? Are there some corrections to the method or the people involved?

Self-sabotage

Make a list of the ways in which you sabotage yourself and what you plan to do to avoid this.

1. ....

....

2. ....

....

3. ....

....

In Summary

My summary of this chapter...

1. ....

2. ....

3. ....

Key Points

1. We can make progress much harder for ourselves through shadow boxing, often subconsciously.
2. Our thoughts and scripts that we run can be investigated and modified – self-acceptance is key.
3. Sticking to our own lives, rather than comparing or being overly interested in others, is a good starting point.

CHAPTER SIXTEEN

Good Daily, Weekly, Monthly and Yearly Habits

Once you have made the leap towards a more meaningful, independent and autonomous Maverick Life, there are some key ideas that can help establish yourself. Sue Ashford from the University of Michigan studied independent workers in 2018 and found four key structures that helped them:

1) Place – defining where and how you work. From experience, this is ideally at home or near home, but not *in* the home – try to have a dedicated workspace that you can 'leave' once your working day is done.
2) Routines – as one participant in Ashford's study put it: 'I do productivity rather than chasing creativity.' She talks about bricklaying, just one layer at a time.
3) Interaction – there need to be other people around that help with affirmation, variety and support – we are not islands.
4) Purpose – reminding yourself why you are doing this new work and the benefits it gives you for the whole of your life.

Many of us shy away from routine and structure, somehow feeling that it inhibits creativity, reduces spontaneity and makes us, dare I say it, *boring*. Mavericks are the opposite. They recognize that having good habits and setting up a routine frees them and multiplies the amount of time they have to do things they want to do. They follow the maxim of

French novelist Gustave Flaubert: 'Be regular and orderly in your life, so that you may be violent and original in your work.'

Let's take a look at effective routines and habits. Not all of these will suit you, so as you read through, circle the ideas that might work.

I was once with a client who announced that he had never learned how to work. It was in the middle of a conversation around discipline and focus. He realized that after a lacklustre education he went straight into running his own business and had never acquired a set of habits or a framework around productivity. He looked on with envy at the Silicon Valley powerhouses who rose at 5 a.m. and had changed the world by 7.30 a.m.

His challenge was that instead of processing all the creative ideas he had, he was deep into a world of distraction through email, social media and the US news cycle. This led to a spiral of feeling helpless, failing to fulfil potential and general escapism. He left the day with a clear plan of how to tackle this and a spring in his step. Here is what we worked through.

The highly productive people I work with structure their days along similar lines. Up at some point between 6 and 7 a.m. Some form of stretching and/or meditation – 10 minutes using an app like Calm is enough at this point. Light breakfast and then a walk or travel to work, thinking about the day ahead. Almost all find mornings their most creative and productive time, some call it the 'morning sprint.' This is typically three to four hours, ending around midday.

Most take some form of short break every 30–45 minutes – a walk around the block or a chat with someone. The morning is absolutely about creating and processing ideas. Doing real work, not responding to or being ruled by inbound calls, emails, meetings or colleagues. This might feel totally impossible in a busy office environment, so perhaps start by trying to carve out 60–90 minutes. Talk to your team and your colleagues: could a group of you experiment with this together? You may have to physically change location for this key work time.

There is then around 45 minutes to an hour of email, WhatsApp and possibly calls. A decent lunch break away from the desk or with someone (ideally 45 minutes) and then the afternoon can be spent in meetings, with a final email session around 4 or 5 p.m. Most seem to finish around 6 or latest 7 p.m. With the morning sprint done there is no need to work late into the night, the productivity boost from working effectively without distraction replaces the two to three hours of poor-quality work done at the end of a long day. Some will exercise before work, others at lunch time or after work. Almost all will take some form of exercise each day, mixing it up with some being fun or low-key interspersed with more high-intensity 'duty' workouts.

My undergrad Psychology dissertation was on the impact of elite sport (rowing) on the academic performance of students. I wanted to debunk the myth that the six hours a day spent training damaged students' grades. The research came back positive – academic achievement was higher among the oarsmen. Why? It was down to time management. With only three to four hours in the morning to work (they were mostly too tired to work in the evenings), the rowers had to be highly productive and disciplined. They had a structured day and routine forced on them and were performing the morning sprint without thinking about it. For those of us who must create our own structure and routines there are rich lessons to be applied.

What do you use for a to-do list? Just as the research shows, goals are more likely to be achieved if written down, so too the tasks associated either with those goals or ongoing daily life. Author and psychologist David Cohen cites three key advantages of the to-do list:

1) They reduce our anxiety about the chaos of life
2) They create a structure for our lives
3) They provide proof of what we have done in the last day or week or month – the joy of ticking something off the list.

You already have an action list in your Maverick Plan (*see also* pages 198–99), now you can combine this with a daily or weekly to-do list and ensure that you are allocating time to both the quarterly goals in your plan and the day-to-day tasks that need to get done. How and where you keep your list is up to you, so experiment and find something that works for you.

Starting the Day

What are your best times of day? Are you a lark or owl? For many of us this is hard to work out because we have never been free enough to establish our natural sleep patterns. Can you think of a time when you were not ruled by an alarm clock and were able to get seven to eight hours' sleep over a few weeks? What happened? Whilst taking a four-month sabbatical, it took a month for my sleep patterns to settle, I was so exhausted. In the end I realized that my natural sleep hours were 10 p.m. to 6 a.m. I was at my best in the morning and increasingly tired from mid-afternoon. Most people are somewhere around this range, although there are those that are hyper-alert in the evening. Understanding your own patterns and working in harmony with them is highly important. Yes, we can train ourselves to go to bed later, but we will not be at our best in the following period.

Morning Routine

How we set up the day has a huge impact. Getting up when the alarm goes (or even better, when you wake up) means a higher energy level. Some form of meditation or reflection where you set up intentions for the day is helpful. Many people journal at this time of day – you could include your intentions or what you hope to get from the day. If you can exercise at this point in the day, the endorphin hit will energize you for the maximum period.

If you are a lark, then your most effective working time – or 'impact hours' as they are called – will be for two to three hours in the morning. Identify these hours when you have the most energy and use them very carefully. This is the time to tackle a difficult task that you have been putting off. Be brutal about picking the right focus here. Timothy Ferriss, author of *The 4-hour Work Week*, famously said, 'Doing something unimportant well does not make it important.'

If you need to tackle something more creative, then now is the time to do it. Most people make the mistake of filling this time with routine tasks like email or unimportant meetings. Protect your precious impact time and be very intentional in how you use it. If you live with others you need to enlist their help and awareness in this. You can turn off phones or other distractions and perhaps find a table or a space that you only use for this purpose.

Breaks

Finding moments during the day to take a break helps keep fatigue at bay, as does moving around. If you have a watch or a phone that keeps track of steps, this is a good way of checking you are not too sedentary. Taking a proper break to eat lunch and read, think or exercise (or all four) makes the afternoon more productive.

Can you find objects or experiences to really savour during the day? Rather than race through everything, take time to sit and be in nature or to focus on a view, a painting or to listen to a piece of music that brings you joy and takes your brain into a different non-work mode. When you are eating rather than just shovelling in fuel, slow down and really notice what you are consuming. In other words, enjoy the moment.

In his book, *Rest: Why You Get More Done When You Work Less*, Alex Soojung-Kim Pang argues that overwork has replaced rest and as a result, our output – particularly our creative output – has fallen. He talks about active rest partnering with work. This is not about lying on the couch rest, instead it might be walking, reading or gardening. He also points out that rest is a lost skill and that highly creative people seem to be excellent at resting. In fact, he argues that deliberate rest makes creativity sustainable.

Pang goes on to suggest that four hours of 'work' is the optimum amount in the day. English naturalist Charles Darwin was always done by noon apparently. Everything that went on around the edges of the four hours – walking, napping, spending time with friends – made those hours more productive. I think most of us have an instinct that working long days over a long period of time makes us far less effective, but four hours a day?

The Pomodoro Technique is a well-known productivity tool that sets up a pattern of 25 minutes of work followed by five-minute breaks. After four of these patterns you can take a longer break of 15–20 minutes. There are simple Pomodoro timers available as apps or for your desktop, search online to find the current recommendations. The key is that when working in a 25-minute sprint, you are absolutely focused and concentrating with no distractions. Hard to do, but very effective if you can train yourself.

End of Day

As the day draws to a close, make sure you are observing the healthy sleep habits from Pillar 2 in Chapter 10 (*see also* page 117). This is also potentially a time to journal, reflecting on what went well and how the day panned out against your intentions. What can you take into tomorrow, what needs attention then? Who might need your help or support tomorrow?

Setting Up a Daily Routine

Pick three daily steps that you would like to work towards in creating a routine for you...

1. ....

....

2. ....

....

3. ....

....

Weekly Routine

In the words of the late CEO and co-founder of St James's Place, Mike Wilson, 'What does a good week look like for you this week?'

What would your perfect week look like? Write a list of all the activities you would like to do in a perfect week and how long you would like to spend on them. Include sleep, spending time with friends and family, alone time, work and all the other stuff. Make this a normal week, not a holiday week. Add up the hours – what do you notice? How is your week split between activities that have meaning for us, that are good for us, that help others and earn us enough to keep our lives going? The Maverick Life creates enough autonomy to choose a balance between self, work and others. How would 30 hours of each look, what would that mean in your life?

What sort of activities are the most beneficial? The New Economics Foundation reviewed the research in 2008 and identified five ways to well-being:

1) Connect – with people around you
2) Be active – get outside, take exercise
3) Take notice – be curious, savour the moment
4) Keep learning – try something new, ask questions
5) Give – do something for others.

They created a bingo game where you go through activities that you enjoy doing and see if you can find one that ticks all five boxes. When I did this exercise, I realized my weekly running club was that. We were a small group, outside in beautiful surroundings, talking and exchanging ideas and advice.

My Perfect Week

Create a list of activities that are important to you to do every week and that tick as many of the criteria above as possible.

Activity	Number of NEF well-being criteria	Best time in the week to do activity

Now put those activities into your diary with a weekly repeat.

Having a day during the week that is a day for researching and thinking, with no meetings, and limited email will completely transform your week. I worked with a CEO who realized that all their best ideas came from their R&D day (research and development day) as they called it. They would do things that they would never normally do during the rest of the week. Go to an art gallery. Meet someone not connected with work. Walk, write, think.

One client was so taken by this idea they named it their 'future Friday' and spent the day thinking about and working on plans and ideas for the future. This follows a well-known rule in Research & Development, which is spend 70 per cent of your time on what is currently working well for you, 20 per cent on evolving and adapting this, and 10 per cent on the moonshot. The problem is many of us spend 110 per cent of our time on a life or a job that is not working well for us, leaving no time to plan and make changes.

Closing the week is important, reviewing how it went compared to what you set out to do. This can also be done on a Friday night around the family table. So, what went well this week? What was a challenge and how did you overcome it? What is a priority for next week? What three things are you grateful for this week?

Monthly, Quarterly and Annual Routine

Following on from the weekly exercise, you then need to review and update the goals that you set back in Chapter 13 in your Maverick Plan (*see also* pages 198–99) on a monthly or quarterly basis. Have a meeting with yourself or even better your accountability partner. Go somewhere different away from distractions. How are you doing against your goals, what needs changing? What do the next few weeks look like, do you need to drop some things or enlist the help of others. Are you basically full? Redo the Life Quotient (LQ) exercise – how have your scores moved? What is moving in the right direction and what might need more work?

A yearly habit that is incredibly effective is going on retreat. Microsoft's Bill Gates takes a reading week, others go silent or on a yoga-heavy week. But we are 110 per cent busy already, I hear you say. How can we possibly find two days to go away, or retreat from our lives? Surely that's just self-indulgence anyway? Even if we can get our heads around this, how do we retreat? Silently? On our own? In a small group or with thousands of others at a large-scale self-help event? How do we know it's going to do us any good, why do we instinctively feel jealous of those that do go 'on retreat'?

In the business world, retreats, or 'offsites' as they are more commonly known, are long established as a chance to step back from the day-to-day firefighting to think more strategically and plan. The most effective companies I work with do this twice a year. The idea is to take time away from working 'in' the business to working 'on' it. Why then would we not apply this to our lives, work on our lives rather than always in our lives?

It is hard to make big decisions on the fly when consumed with the demands of email, work, family and friends. It is also hard to make big decisions on your own, to gain the clarity that enables a good decision or change to be made. It is hard to make plans while we are just getting through the days, hard to figure out what is making us feel restless, anxious and just a bit 'off'. All of this leads me to strongly suggest you find a way at least once a year to take one to two days out to work on *you*. In his book, *The Art of Loving*, psychologist Erich Fromm argues that 'only a person who has faith in himself can be faithful to others'. Essentially, he is pointing out that unless you love yourself and look after yourself first, there is no way of being of service to others in the long term.

Without *you* there is no one else – no Maverick, no relationships or impact in your community. Does going on retreat still seem self-indulgent? No, it seems like an absolute necessity. Being available and showing up for others properly means having your own house in order first.

I have just finished leading a two-day Maverick retreat for six people. The whole experience was incredibly powerful for the group and me. What struck me was watching them bond so quickly and move to help each other in ways I could not have predicted. While I provided structure, some knowledge and ongoing challenge, much of the impact came from within them. Working in different pairs throughout the retreat, they all found this short experience to be life changing. They looked at defining their life purpose, improving their own performance (around eating, sleep, exercise and state of mind) and finally at the key relationships in their lives.

This was made more intense by everyone handing their phones in at the start. A two-day tech break ensured that everyone was present in a way they had forgotten how to be, totally without compromise – although it also meant no one turned up for breakfast as no phones meant no alarm clocks.

While I have no doubt that silent, solo or large group retreats have huge value, I was somehow not prepared for the power of a small group working with a facilitator. I had already coached some of the participants in a 1-2-1 environment and it quickly became clear they were gaining insights from the group that were not available in our sessions. The combination of individual and group work emerged as highly compelling.

This is not necessarily a plug to retreat with Haddon Coaching, but a plug to retreat full stop. Even walking for three hours with a friend or your dog is a form of retreat. Creating and taking space allows our minds and bodies the latitude to work on the knotty issues lurking under the stormwater of daily life. Some preparation beforehand can really help make the most of your retreat time.

What feels realistic for you? Half a day, an overnight? On your own or with a friend? Organized by someone else or by you? Where will you go? What matters is that you reach for your diary – now – and block out some time and commit to retreating. Give yourself the gift of creating the future you want.

Monthly and Yearly Routines

You have designed a daily and weekly routine already. Now it's time to write down what you want to do on a monthly, quarterly and yearly basis.

Monthly

....

....

....

....

Quarterly

....

....

....

....

Yearly

....

....

....

....

In Summary

My summary of this chapter…

1. ……………………………………………………

2. ……………………………………………………

3. ……………………………………………………

Key Points

1. If you are working from home, setting up a location and good habits are crucial.

2. Establishing a routine increases productivity and creativity, allowing time for pleasurable activities.

3. Finding time to retreat on a small regular basis and on a longer basis once a year allows you to keep your Maverick Life on track.

CHAPTER SEVENTEEN

A Call to Action

Congratulations, you really have stuck at this and made it to the end of the book. If I was in the room with you, we would hug and celebrate, we would also talk about how to make your ideas and plans happen, rather than languish in a journal or on a to-do list.

You began by looking at yourself to understand some of the key building blocks of who you are and what makes you tick. Your Life Quotient (LQ) score gave you some early indicators as to what might be keeping your battery levels low. Next, you took the blinkers off and engaged with what was possible. You dared to dream about the life you really wanted. Then you worked on building your scaffolding that underpins the next chapter of your life. Finally, you looked at how to maintain forward progress, creating good habits – shortcuts, if you like.

The real challenge starts now.

Contemplating and making changes requires energy, resolve and space. Work on some of the key pillars. If I had to suggest one, then Pillar 2: Sleep (*see also* pages 116–20) would be a place to start. Clear thinking, decision making and forward progress are practically impossible without a good sleep reserve. A second area for quick results would be Pillar 4: Exercise (*see also* pages 125–28). Walking 30 minutes a day gives a major boost to your thinking and energy levels. Both are quick wins and help put you on your new path.

> 'I believe that drudgery and clock-watching are a terrible betrayal of that universal, inborn entrepreneurial spirit.' *Richard Branson*

Please don't let this be you. It's time to engage your entrepreneurial spirit – if you have read this far, then you are likely to be of that mindset. Take one of your goals, one that you have confidence you can do. Pick someone to make yourself accountable to and arrange to meet with them or check in with them in a few days or a few weeks depending on the goal. If things go wrong, be interested rather than judgemental of yourself. Fail well and come back wiser.

Once you have started turning the flywheel and achieved your aim, it becomes addictive. Living the life you love, the life you believe in and want, the life you know you are capable of creates its own energy; the flywheel starts turning faster and faster. Over time the effort you need to put in reduces. Habits form, your batteries stay full, energy is high and focused on areas that bring you and those around you joy and meaning.

Check-in

So how are you feeling? Write down what is in your head and heart right now:

....

....

....

....

....

This simple question tells us so much about what is going on inside us. I hope you are feeling energized and excited, if a little daunted or overwhelmed. You have already made huge progress as you have worked through this book. You have just completed your last exercise too. Many congratulations. The Maverick Path recognizes that none of this is easy, it all takes time and society puts major obstacles in our path.

There are people to help you. You have identified many of these people as you have completed the exercises. There are Maverick coaches who can help you on a 1-2-1 basis. There are Maverick retreats where you can join a small group with coaches to help you turbo-charge your Maverick path. There is also the Maverick community, all of which you can find at www.themodernmaverick.com. Accountability is a key driver of change so working with others in your own world or engaging in the Maverick community will transform your ability to make the changes you want to.

In the past working on ourselves has sometimes seemed self-indulgent. Now with the world in a perilous state it is compulsory. We all need to be at our best, engaged in our purpose and energetically pursuing it. With a world full of Mavericks, we can and will prosper. Of course, our economies will grow and endure recessions, and our standard of living will improve but that will be a secondary output. The main win will be us living in our communities in harmony with our environment.

I know there is a lot to take in. The book is dense with ideas and questions. If you are feeling overwhelmed that is totally understandable. Trying to do it all will result in procrastination. It takes real courage to look inside yourself; start with something small, that you are excited to do, that feels within reach. Momentum builds momentum and feels wonderful. Expect setbacks, and periods of low activity. Just keep moving forwards.

When you finish reading this paragraph, your Maverick Plan is complete. Go back through the book and pull out highlights. Create your own scrapbook if you like, feel free to get the scissors and glue stick out. Good luck, I know you can do it. Please let me know how you go at the Modern Maverick website. We are all here to support each other. It has been a privilege working with you. Welcome to the Maverick Movement, a movement of collective individualism.

In Summary

My summary of this chapter…

1. ....

2. ....

3. ....

Key Points

1. The brain needs a clear plan and a set of goals to create forward momentum.
2. Finding and meeting with an accountability partner is essential in making the plan a reality.
3. Using Key Performance Indicators (KPIs) to make an honest assessment and course correction is a normal and critical part of executing a successful plan.
4. Change is hard; understanding the key stages of change and the power of habits can help progress.
5. We need to build up our key change muscles of resilience and willpower.
6. Focusing on and completing a key action is the best way to start on your Maverick Path.
7. We can make progress much harder for ourselves through shadow boxing, often subconsciously.
8. Our thoughts and scripts that we run can be investigated and modified; self-acceptance is key.
9. Sticking to our own lives, rather than comparing to or being overly interested in others, is a good starting point.
10. If you are working from home, setting up a location and good habits are crucial.

11. Establishing a routine increases productivity and creativity, allowing time for pleasurable activities.

12. Finding time to retreat on a small regular basis and on a longer basis once a year allows you to keep your Maverick Life on track.

13. Well done for finishing the book, you have laid the foundations and now the work to make it real begins.

14. Please just start, pick a goal or a change you want to make and go for it.

15. There is a community and Maverick Coaches out there to support you – search for The Modern Maverick online.

Appendix: 80th Birthday Visualization Script

Slow, hypnotic voice with plenty of pauses:

I'd like you to close your eyes or allow your eyes to go into peripheral vision and soften your gaze and the muscles in your face, whichever is most comfortable for you.

Just allow your breathing to deepen, taking your breath now down from your chest area to your tummy. By changing our breath we change our state and by slowing our breathing we allow our minds to enter a space where creativity and ideas can come and go, a bit like just before we fall asleep at night, where our brainwaves relax into a different state.

This is time now for you to switch off from the day-to-day concerns and spend a little bit of time thinking about your future; any thoughts that are bubbling to the surface now, allow yourself to put them away.

Imagine locking them in a box in a room, knowing that they are safe there until you are ready to access them later on today. Things on the to-do list, ideas, noises from outside, any distractions... just pop them away for now, knowing you can come back to them later today.

As you start to relax, you may notice sounds inside and outside the room you had not noticed before, and that's OK and they are not important right now, just let them wash over you.

I am going to invite you, in just a minute, to imagine that you are celebrating a landmark birthday. In full health and feeling incredibly proud of the life choices you have made. I want you to imagine now that you are celebrating your 80th birthday.

Now, take a few moments to notice where this wonderful celebration is taking place. You are in full health, feeling positive about the life you have lived so far. Take a few moments to notice where you are... It may be somewhere you have always wanted to go but never been, it may be somewhere that you have always longed to go… or it may be somewhere that you already know and love…

…and maybe someone organized this for you or maybe you organized it yourself, but just take a few moments to appreciate and notice the sights and sounds and tastes as you look around at the venue of this special event.

Notice also the smells and tastes of the food and drinks that are part of the celebration and the sounds and sights of all the people that are there.

Take a few moments now to notice who is there, the way they look, the sound of their laughter and chatter, the feel of their hugs.

Maybe there are some surprises about who is there or maybe there are no surprises at all…

…And maybe one of those people makes a speech about you.

Listen to what they are saying about you, the adjectives they use to describe you and the impact you have had on their life and lives around you. The funny stories they tell about you and the anecdotes they use to describe the contribution you have made…

...And maybe you make a speech yourself or maybe you are just quietly reflecting on your life as you look over the last 80 years.

...As you think about what you learned in each decade and what was important.

As you think about your 70s, who and what was important, where and how were you spending your time?

The highs and lows, what lessons you learned?

What choices you made?

Who and what mattered?

And how this was the same or different to your 60s.

As you think about your 60s, who and what were important?

Where and how were you spending your time?

The highs and lows, what lessons you learned, what choices you took?

Who and what mattered?
How was this the same or different to your 50s?
As you think about your 50s, who and what was important?
Where and how were you spending your time?
The highs and lows, what lessons you learned, what choices you took?
Who and what mattered?
And how this was the same or different to your 40s.
As you think about your 40s, who and what was important?
Where and how were you spending your time?
The highs and lows, what lessons you learned, what choices you took?
Who and what mattered?
And how this was the same or different to your 30s.
As you think about your 30s, who and what was important?
Where and how were you spending your time?
The highs and lows, what lessons you learned, what choices you took?
Who and what mattered?
And how this was the same or different to your 20s, your first decade of independent, adult life.
As you think about your 20s, who and what was important?
Where and how were you spending your time?
The highs and lows, what lessons you learned, what choices you took?
Who and what mattered?

And as you reflect over all the decades and the learning and wisdom you have acquired, offer a piece of wisdom from your 80-year-old self to your current self today with all the choices and decisions they are facing.

One piece of advice.

One piece of wisdom.

And then when you are ready, take a long look around at the people and the celebration and take what you need with you as you return to the here and now, feeling totally refreshed and alert.

With kind permission from Fiona Parashar.

Parashar, P. *A Beautiful Way to Coach: Positive Psychology Coaching in Nature*. London (UK): Routledge (2022).

References and Bibliography

Note: items in **bold** are recommended for further reading

Chapter 2. Key Moments and What They Tell You

Lyubomirsky, S. *The How of Happiness: A Practical Guide to Getting the Life You Want*. London (UK): Piatkus (2007).

Further reading around ACEs at www.acestoohigh.com

Ben-Shahar, T. *How to be Happier* video interview with Mark Williamson. London (UK): Action for Happiness (2020).

Jobs, S. Commencement Speech at Stanford University. Stanford (US): *Stanford News* (2005).

Whyte, D. *River Flow: New and Selected Poems, 1984–2007*. Langley (Washington): Many Rivers Press (2007).

Chapter 3: What Matters to You?

Gladwell, M. *The Tipping Point: How Little Things Can Make a Big Difference*. New York (US): Little, Brown and Company (2000).

Chapter 4: The LQ Self-Discovery Scale

Gilbert, D. *Stumbling on Happiness*. New York (US): Alfred A. Knopf (2006).

Chapter 6: Defining Your Own Version of Success

UK statistic for shares owned from *Finder* article by Charlie Barton, 4 August 2021. US statistic from Gallup survey updated on 13 August 2021.

Ware, B. *The Top 5 Regrets of the Dying: A Life Transformed by the Dearly Departing*. London (UK): Hay House (2019).

Set point of happiness theory supported by research such as Brickman, P., Coates, D. and Janoff-Bulman, R. 'Lottery winners and accident victims: Is happiness relative?' *Journal of Personality and Social Psychology*, 36(8), 917–927 (1978).

Vaillant, G.E. *Triumphs of Experience: The Men of the Harvard Grant Study*. The Belknap Press of Harvard University Press (2012).

www.willitmaketheboatgofaster.com

Book coach is at https://alisonjones.com

Chapter 7: Figuring Out Your Purpose

Sinek, S. *Start with Why: How Great Leaders Inspire Everyone to Take Action.* New York (US): Portfolio (2009).

Steptoe, A., Deaton, A. and Stone, A.A. 'Subjective well-being, health and ageing'. *Lancet* (2015).

Chapter 8: A First Look at the Life You Want

Richo, D. *The Five Longings: What We've Always Wanted – and Already Have.* US: Shambhala Publications Inc. (2017).

Chapter 9: The Maverick Path

Working hour statistics from www.statista.com

Deci, L. and Ryan, R. *Intrinsic Motivation and Self-Determination in Human Behavior*. New York: Plenum (1985).

Kukita, A., Nakamura, J. and Csikszentmihalyi, M. 'How experiencing autonomy contributes to a good life', *The Journal of Positive Psychology*, 17:1, 34–45 (2022).

Steckermeier, L. 'The value of autonomy for a good life. An empirical investigation of Autonomy and life satisfaction in Europe', Social Indicators research. Springer (2020).

Yin-Yang, L. 'Do patient autonomy preferences matter? Linking patient-centred care to patient-physician relationships and health outcomes'. *Social Science and Medicine*, volume 71, issue 10. Elsevier (2010).

Warr, P. and Inceoglu, I. 'Work orientations, well-being and job content of self-employed and employed professionals.' *Journal of Work, Employment and Society*. Sage Journals (2017).

PWC 2016. 'Work-life 3.0: Understanding how we'll work next'. *Consumer Intelligence Series*. PWC.com/CISworklife

Berg, J., Dutton, J. and Wrzesniewski, A. 'What is job crafting and why does it matter?' Center for Positive Organisational Scholarship. Michigan School of Business (2008).

Morrow-Howell, N., Hinterlong, J., Rozario, P. and Tang, F. 'Effects of Volunteering on the Well-Being of Older Adults'. *The Journals of Gerontology Series B*, volume 58, issue 3, May 2003, pp. S137–S145.

Friedman, H. and Martin, L. 'The Longevity Project: Surprising discoveries for health and long life from the landmark eight-decade study'. US: Plume (2012).

https://www.nhs.uk/live-well/exercise/exercise-health-benefits

Lyubomirsky S., Lepper HS: A measure of subjective happiness: Preliminary reliability and construct validation. Soc Indicators Res. 1999, 46(2): 137–155.

Chapter 10: Self

Grant, A. 'Solution-focused cognitive behavioural coaching for sustainable high performance and circumventing stress, fatigue and burnout'. *Consulting Psychology Journal: Practice and Research*, 69(2), 98–111 (2017).

Heekerens, J. and Eid, M. 'Inducing positive affect and positive future expectations using the best possible self-intervention: A systematic review and meta-analysis'. *The Journal of Positive Psychology*. Advance online publication (2020).

Seligman, M. *Learned Optimism: How to Change Your Mind and Your Life*. US: Vintage (2006).

ISMA survey at www.isma.org.uk

Blackburn, E. and Epel, E. *The Telemore Effect: The New Science of Living Younger*. New York (US): Grand Central Publishing (2017).

University of Warwick. 'Lack of Sleep Doubles Risk of Death, But So Can Too Much Sleep'. *ScienceDaily*, 24 September 2007.

Useful Apps for meditation – Calm, Headspace, Waking Up.

Walker, M. *Why We Sleep*. London (UK): Penguin Books (2018).

Limbana, T., Khan, F. and Eskander, N. *Gut Microbiome and Depression: How Microbes Affect the Way We Think*. Cureus. Published online, August 2020.

Mosley, M. *The Fast Diet: Revised and Updated: Lose Weight, Stay Healthy, Live Longer*. London (UK): Short Books (2014).

Functional capacity chart adapted from Kalache, A. and Kickbush, I. 'A global strategy for healthy ageing'. *World Health*, 50(4): 5 (1997).

Health benefits of exercise at www.nhs.uk/live-well/exercise/exercise-health-benefits/

Chapter 11: Others

Ford, B. and colleagues. 'Culture shapes whether the pursuit of happiness predicts higher or lower well-being'. *Journal of Experimental Psychology*. 144(6): 1053–62 (2015).

Alexander, B.K., Beyerstein, B.L., Hadaway, P.F. and Coambs, R.B. 'Effect of early and later colony housing on oral ingestion of morphine in rats'. *Pharmacol Biochem Behav*. 1981 Oct;15(4):571–6. doi: 10.1016/0091-3057(81)90211-2. PMID: 7291261.

Alison, E. and Alison, L. *Rapport: The Four Ways to Read People*. London (UK): Vermilion (2020).

Benson, H. and Benson, K. *What Mums Want (and Dads Need to Know)*. UK: Lion Books (2017).

Gottman, J. *The Seven Principles for Making Marriage Work: A Practical Guide From the International Bestselling Relationship Expert*. US: Orion Spring (2018).

Champan, G. *The 5 Love Languages: The Secret to Love That Lasts*. US: Moody Publishers (2015).

Lyubomirsky, S. *The How of Happiness: A New Approach to Getting the Life You Want*. London (UK): Piatkus (2007).

Biddulph, S. *Raising Boys: Why Boys are Different – And How to Help Them Become Happy and Well-balanced Men*. US: Harper Thorson (2003).

Young Minds. 'Childhood adversity, substance misuse and young people's mental health'. Published online by Young Minds and Add Addiction (2018).

Layard, R., Clark, A., Cornaglia, F., Powdthavee, N. and Vernoit, J. 'What predicts a successful life? A life-course model of well-being'. London (UK): LSE consulting (2013).

Faber, A. and Mazlish, E. *How to Talk so Kids Will Listen & Listen so Kids Will Talk*. New York (US): Scribner (2012).

Ivanova, D., Barrett, J., Wiedenhofer, D., Macura, B., Callaghan, M. and Creutzig, F. 'Quantifying the potential for climate change mitigation of consumption options'. Environmental Research Letters (2020).

Chenoweth, E. and Stephan, J. *Why Civil Resistance Works: The Strategic Logic of Nonviolent Conflict*. US: Columbia University Press (2011).

Chapter 12: Work

Gallup. *State of the Global Workplace*. New York (US): Gallup Press (2017).

Schwartz, B. *The Paradox of Choice: Why More is Less*. US: Harper Perennial (2005).

Krznaric, R. *How to Find Fulfilling Work*. New York (US): Picador (2013).

Wickman, G. and Winters, M. *Rocket Fuel: The One Essential Combination That Will Get You More of What You Want From Your Business*. US: BenBella Books (2021).

Kahneman, D. and Deaton, A. 'High income improves evaluation of life but not emotional well-being'. US: Proceedings of the National Academy of Sciences, volume 107, issue 38 (2010).

Killingsworth, M. 'Experienced well-being rises with income even above $75,000 per year'. US: *Psychological and Cognitive Sciences*, https://doi.org/10.1073/pnas.2016976118 (2021).

Smeets, P., Whillans, A. and Bekkers, R. 'Time Use and Happiness for Millionaires: Evidence from the Netherlands'. US: *Social Psychological and Personality Science*, volume 11, issue 3, 295–307 (2019).

Benson, H. and Azim, R. 'Celebrity Divorce Rates'. UK: The Marriage Foundation, published online at www.marriagefoundation.org.uk (2016).

Alcaraz, P. *The Wealth Game: An Ordinary Person's Companion*. UK: Hutchinson Reed. With permission to include the level of detail from the book (2015).

Raser-Rowland, A. and Grubb, A. *The Art of Frugal Hedonism: A Guide to Spending Less While Enjoying Everything More*. US: Melliodora Publishing (2021).

Dunn, E., Aknin, L. and Norton, M. 'Spending Money on Others Promotes Happiness'. *Science*, 319, no. 5870, 1687–1688 (2008).

Net worth of Bill Gates at 4 May 2022: £125bn. Source: Bloomberg.com

Median net worth of American households: $121,760 in 2019. Source: Federal Reserve.

Allen, D. *Getting Things Done: The Art of Stress-free Productivity*. US: Piatkus (2015).

De Gusta, M. Are Smartphones Spreading Faster than Any Technology in Human History? US: *MIT Technology Review* (2012).

Consumer Insights Microsoft Canada. 'Attention Spans'. (2015).

Duke, K., Ward, A., Gneezy, A. and Bos, M. 'Having your smartphone nearby takes a toll on your thinking'. US: *Harvard Business Review* (2018).

Chapter 13: Your Maverick Plan

Association for Talent Development research referenced in article; Wissman, B. 'An accountability partner makes you vastly more likely to succeed'. Entrepneur.com (2018).

Beveridge, H. and Hunt-Davis, B. *Will It Make the Boat Go Faster? Olympic-winning Strategies for Everyday Success*, Second Edition. UK: Troubador (2020).

Dalai Lama (Tenzin Gyatso) and Tutu, D. *The Book of Joy: Lasting Happiness in a Changing World.* With Douglas Abrams. New York (US): Avery (2016).

Christensen, C., Allworth, J. and Dillon, K. *How Will You Measure Your Life?*, New York (US): HarperBusiness (2012).

Chapter 14: Making Effective Changes

Prochaska, J. and DiClemente, C. 'Stages and processes of self-change of smoking: Toward an integrative model of change'. *Journal of Consulting and Clinical Psychology*, 51(3), 390–395. http://dx.doi.org/10.1037/0022-006X.51.3.390 (1983).

Duhigg, C. *The Power of Habit: Why We Do What We Do and How to Change.* US: Random House (2012).

Prochaska, J. referenced on p.109 of *The Power of Habit.*

Kaiser Permanente (8 July 2008). 'Keeping A Food Diary Doubles Diet Weight Loss, Study Suggests'. *ScienceDaily.*

Muraven, M. and Baumeister, R. 'Self-regulation and depletion of limited resources: Does self-control resemble a muscle?' *Psychological Bulletin,* 126, 247–259 (2000).

de Shazer, S. *Clues: Investigating Solutions in Brief Therapy*. US: W. W. Norton & Co. (1988).

Chapter 15: Staying Out of Your Own Way

Baumeister, R. and Tierney, J. *Willpower: Rediscovering the Greatest Human Strength*. New York (US): Penguin (2011).

Dweck, C. *Mindset: The New Psychology of Success*. New York (US): Random House (2006).

Persuad, R. *The Motivated Mind*. London (UK): Bantham (2005).

Chapter 16: Good Daily, Weekly, Monthly and Yearly Habits

Petriglieri, G., Ashford, S. and Wrzesniewski, A. 'Agony and Ecstasy in the Gig Economy: Cultivating Holding Environments for Precarious and Personalized Work Identities'. *Administrative Science Quarterly*, 64 (2018).

Pang, A. *Rest: Why You Get More Done When You Work Less*. US: Basic Books (2016).

Ferriss, T. *The 4-Hour Work Week: Escape the 9–5, Live Anywhere and Join the New Rich*. US: Vermillion (2011).

Aked, J., Cordon, C., Marks, N. and Thompson, S. 'Five ways to well-being: A report presented to the Foresight project on communicating the evidence base for improving people's well-being'. London (UK): New Economics Foundation (2008).

David Cohen interviewed in the *Guardian* newspaper by Louise Chunn, 10 May 2017.

Fromm, E. *The Art of Loving*. New York (US): Perennial Library (1989).

Chapter 17: A Call to Action

www.themodernmaverick.com

Index